FERGUSON
CAREER BIOGRAPHIES

LANCE
ARMSTRONG

Cyclist

Michael Benson

Ferguson
An imprint of ☑ Facts On File

Lance Armstrong: Cyclist

Copyright © 2004 by Ferguson

Ferguson
An imprint of Facts On File, Inc.
132 West 31st Street
New York NY 10001

Benson, Michael.
  Lance Armstrong, cyclist/Michael Benson
    p. cm. — (Ferguson career biographies)
Includes index.
Summary: A biography of sports superstar Lance Armstrong, known both for repeatedly winning the prestigious, long-distance bicycle race, the Tour de France, and for surviving cancer.
  ISBN 0-8160-5479-7 (hc: alk. paper)
    1. Armstrong, Lance—Juvenile literature. 2. Cyclists—United States—Biography—Juvenile literature. [1. Armstrong, Lance. 2. Cyclists. 3. Cancer—Patients.] I. Title. II. Series.

GV1051.A76B46 2003
796.6'2'092—dc22   2003015339

Ferguson books are available at special discounts when purchased in bulk quantities for businesses, associations, institutions, or sales promotions. Please call our Special Sales Department in New York at (212) 967-8800 or (800) 322-8755.

You can find Ferguson on the World Wide Web at http://www.fergpubco.com

Text design by David Strelecky

Pages 103–132 adapted from Ferguson's *Encyclopedia of Careers and Vocational Guidance, Twelfth Edition*

Printed in the United States of America

MP FOF 10 9 8 7 6 5 4 3 2 1

This book is printed on acid-free paper.

CONTENTS

1

FIGHT TO WIN, FIGHT TO LIVE

Lance Armstrong has become a sports legend in the United States. Although there is no shortage of legends and superstars in such popular U.S. sports as football, basketball, and baseball, Armstrong is different. He became a legend, a superstar, in a sport that wasn't very popular at all in the U.S.—at least not until he began to dominate it. Lance is a long-distance bicycle racer, known for his consecutive victories of the most famous long-distance bicycle race of all, the Tour de France.

These victories alone are enough to make Lance Armstrong a one-of-a-kind athlete, but there is more to his story. Before he could become a legendary cyclist, Lance had to come back from a near-fatal illness. He has proven time and again that there is no end to his toughness, no end to his determination. In the process he has become an inspiration both to those who fight to win, and to those who must fight to live.

Lance Armstrong at the 1999 Tour de France. (Corbis)

"TURN EVERY NEGATIVE INTO A POSITIVE"

Lance Armstrong was born on September 18, 1971, near Dallas, Texas. He was a big baby, weighing nine pounds, 12 ounces. Lance's mother, Linda Mooneyham, was only 17 when he was born. Lance's mother and father were married when Linda was pregnant, but they had broken up and Lance's father left by the time Lance was born. Lance never asked about his father, and his mother never told him. Although later in life Lance would learn more about his father from a newspaper reporter, he had no interest in meeting him. As far as Lance is concerned, he has only one parent, his devoted mother Linda.

When he was a baby, Lance and his mother shared a small apartment in a run-down suburb of Dallas called Oak Cliff. His mom worked a series of low-paying jobs—at a grocery store, a fast-food restaurant—to make ends meet. Lance was at child-care during the day, but at night his mother paid a lot of attention to him. She wanted him to always know that he was wanted—and he did. They played games and every night she read a book to him.

Lance did show signs of being a world-class athlete even as a baby. He started to walk when he was only nine months old.

Things got a little better for Lance and his mom when he was a toddler. She quit her store and restaurant jobs and got a new, better-paying job as a secretary. (Today, Lance's mother is both an account manager in an office and a real-estate salesperson.)

Linda was Lance's best friend and biggest supporter when he was growing up. "Turn every negative into a positive," was her motto, and it soon became Lance's as well.

A New Stepfather

When Lance was three, his mother married a man named Terry Armstrong. Although, Lance and Terry never got along, Terry legally adopted Lance, changing Lance's last name to Armstrong. Lance describes Terry as being "every cliché of a traveling salesman." That is, he thought of

Terry as a liar who had trouble staying in one place. Soon after Terry and Linda were married, the family moved to the nicer Dallas suburb of Plano.

Lance had good reasons for not liking his stepfather. Terry used to beat Lance with a paddle over minor things—like not cleaning up his room or spilling his milk. And, even worse, once when Linda was in the hospital having an operation, Lance caught Terry writing love letters to another woman.

First Bike

Lance got his first bicycle when he was seven years old. The bike came from a bike shop directly across the street from his apartment. The owner of the store, a man named Jim Hoyt, sponsored bike races and teams. Lance looked like an athletic kid so, seeing a future cyclist, Hoyt gave Lance's mom a deal on a bike. Lance's first bicycle was a brown Schwinn Mag Scrambler with yellow wheels. It wasn't a beauty but Lance loved it.

In Plano, the sport of choice was football. The Plano high school was one of the largest in Texas, and its football players were heroes. Lance tried to play football but he wasn't very good at it. By the time he got to high school he knew that trying out for the team was out of the question.

Lance got his first taste of athletic success in the fifth grade. That year his elementary school held a long-distance running race. Before the race Lance's mother gave him a 1972 silver dollar and told him the coin would bring him luck. Lance entered and won the race. He soon discovered that he was talented at anything that involved moving forward over long distances, in spite of whether the competition left him tired or in tremendous pain.

Everyone in the Pool

That same year he joined a swimming club. At first he was not a good swimmer, thrashing and splashing while staying pretty much in one place. But he was determined to get better at it—and he did.

It was at this time that Lance first learned to train hard. He found that if you want to excel at something you have to do it again and again. He also found that if the activity involves racing, you have to do it more than the people you will be racing against.

Before long Lance was an excellent swimmer. In less than a year in the swimming club, he became one of the best swimmers in Texas, and finished fourth in the state in a 1,500-meter freestyle race.

During that year he was swimming six miles a day. And, since the pool was 10 miles from his home, and he rode his bike to and from practice, he was biking 20 miles a day on top of that.

Becoming a Triathlete

In 1984, when Lance was 13, he learned about a form of racing that seemed designed just for him. It was called the triathlon. A triathlon is three long-distance races in one. It starts out with a long swim, then a long bicycle race, immediately followed by a long foot race. Lance saw an advertisement for an upcoming triathlon for young athletes called Iron Kids, and he signed up to race. His mother bought him a triathlon outfit made out of fast-drying material, and he got his first racing bike, a Mercier. It was no contest. Lance won the junior triathlon by a wide margin. The second- and third-place finishers were specks in the distance when Lance crossed the finish line. He soon signed up to race in a second triathlon in Houston, and again he won by a large margin.

Whether it was because he was unhappy living under the same roof as Terry Armstrong, or perhaps because he was 13 years old, during this time in his life, Lance was a discipline problem. He was reckless and did dangerous, even foolish, things. Perhaps the most foolish game he ever played was called "fireball." He and a friend would soak tennis balls in kerosene, light them on fire, and play catch with them while wearing oven mittens. Lance set off one major explosion and almost burned down a neighbor's house before he retired from the sport. Soon after the fireball phase, Linda separated from Terry. Lance was much

A competitor in the Iron Kids Triathlon. Lance competed in the event when he was 13. (Photo courtesy of brightroom.com)

happier with Terry gone. His mother was more relaxed as well. He never lost his taste for excitement and doing things fast, but he did promise his mom he would stop misbehaving.

Until the age of 15 Lance had always raced against other teenagers and he had always won. But when he was 15 he raced for the first time against adults who were experienced athletes. (The race rules said that you had to be 16 to compete, but Lance added a year to his age on the application.) The event was the 1987 President's Triathlon in Lake Lavon, Texas. He only finished in 32d place, but spectators and reporters at the race were amazed that he had finished at all. After the race Lance told one newspaperman: "I think in a few years I'll be right near the top, and within 10 years I'll be the best."

As a cyclist, Lance was maturing quickly. When he raced in the 1988 President's Triathlon, his performance greatly improved. From 32d place the previous year, he pushed his way up toward the front and finished fifth at age 16.

Valuable Lessons

Not all of Lance's maturity was a result of his getting bigger and stronger. He was getting smarter, as well. One lesson that Lance learned the hard way was how to eat properly. He learned that his body was a racing machine and if he didn't give it the proper fuel, it wasn't going to perform up to its capabilities.

Once when he was 15, Lance ate two cinnamon rolls and drank a soda before a race. In the middle of the race Lance felt his energy drop until he felt like he was going to fall over. The other racers passed him as if he were standing still. In the racing business, this is called "bonking." It's like a car that runs out of gas. Because his mother had taught him to never quit, he ended up walking across the finish line. It was the last time he was careless about his nutrition before competing.

One of the best things about being a triathlete was that it was a professional sport. Every time Lance finished a race near the front, he received a check. At age 16, Lance made $20,000 from different types of racing.

In addition to triathlons, Lance also competed in bike races. Jim Hoyt, the bike-store owner who had sold Lance his first bicycle, also sponsored a bicycle racing team that competed in weekly local races. Lance joined Hoyt's team and started out competing against other teenagers. He won the races easily. Soon he was training with and racing against grown men. It was Hoyt who taught Lance how important it was to control his temper during races. Once Lance got into a fight with another racer after a hard race and Hoyt took his bicycle away. He refused to return the bike until Lance agreed that fighting and racing did not mix.

Lance trained for bike races the same way he did everything: hard and long. He would ride his bike at 30 miles per hour for many hours a day. To illustrate how much Lance punished his body, he would burn 6,000 calories—about the same number of calories most people eat in three days—and sweat out 10 quarts of water during a training session. Lance was a thirsty and hungry guy when he finally got off his bike.

Racing as a Job

Before long, Lance stopped thinking of racing as just a sport. He began to think of it as a job and, soon enough, as a career. Lance was ahead of his time, as most Americans didn't even know there was such a thing as professional bicycle racers until 1986, when American Greg LeMond won the Tour de France.

Lance didn't just practice and race. In addition to his six-mile run, laps in the pool, and hours on his bike, he also kept a file of the names and phone numbers of men and women who sponsored cyclists and race competitions. He called this his file of "business contacts."

Sponsors were people who would pay Lance's travel expenses and put him up in a hotel room if he wore the name of their company on his uniform when he raced. If he won and was interviewed by reporters, Lance was expected to mention the name of his sponsor as often as possible. The sponsors thought of him as a commercial on wheels.

Lance was successful enough to buy himself a sports car while still in high school. (Naturally, given his love of speed, he drove it way too fast.) Despite his many accomplishments, he still didn't fit in with the other kids at his high school, most of whom were very fashion conscious. At Plano's high school you had to wear the right clothes if you wanted to run with the in-crowd. But Lance wasn't concerned with what he wore—a point he once proved at a 12-mile bike race. The weather was colder than he had expected, and he ended up wearing his mother's pink jacket. He still had the jacket on as he crossed the finish line in first place, breaking the old course record by 45 seconds.

Nor did Lance mind if people thought he was a little crazy. He went on a camping trip 60 miles from home with some friends in high school. He took his bike with him. When the others packed up their gear for the drive home, Lance declined. He said he would bike it, all 60 miles. Sometimes he would train so hard on Saturdays that his rides would take him to the Oklahoma border. On these occasions, unable to make it home before dinner, he would call his mother to come pick him up in the car.

Of the three types of races in a triathlon, Lance liked bicycling the best. By the time he was a senior in high school, he was limiting his training to bicycling only.

Traffic Troubles

During his teenage years, Lance learned that training could be extremely difficult and demanding, and not just in a physical sense. There are many outside factors that can make training to be a cyclist a very treacherous activity.

For example, Lance learned not to go out on his bike alone. If he did get hit by a car and seriously injured, he did not want to be stranded by the side of the road. Lance always had a friend following behind in a car, in order to keep an eye on him.

The open road can also be a painful road, as gravel and debris often cuts or gets stuck in a cyclist's legs. Since wounds are easier to clean and bandage if there is no hair, Lance began to shave his legs, just as all professional cyclists do.

As Lance also learned, perhaps the biggest hazard of cycling is sharing the road with cars and trucks. Lance has lost count of the number of times he has been hit by a motor vehicle. There are scars on his arms and legs from these accidents. He was hurt so frequently in this way that he learned how to take out his own stitches.

Some drivers do drive around Lance, but that does not mean they are happy about it. He is shouted at and insulted, and has had many things thrown at him, including glass bottles. Truck drivers have tried to park their trucks across the road to block his path, but Lance has always found room to go around. And he will never forget the time a driver passed him, pulled over on the shoulder of the road, and then got out and started swinging a baseball bat.

Lance's first bad experience with a truck came when he was still a teenager. The truck ran him off the road and Lance cursed at the driver. The driver stopped the truck and threw a gas can at Lance. Lance ran away, leaving his bike by the side of the road. The driver stomped on the bike before getting back into his truck and driving away. Lance got the driver's license plate number, however, and his mother sued the driver for the cost of the bike and bought Lance a new bicycle with the money.

That first incident was purely the driver's fault, but that was not always the case. Not long after the incident with the truck, Lance was "playing chicken" in traffic. He was running red lights, trying to get through intersections before the cars crossing his path hit him. That is a very dangerous game—both for the cyclists and motorists. One day he shot into the path of a woman in a Ford Bronco. Lance was sent flying off his bike. He was not wearing a helmet and he landed headfirst in a heap at the curb. His head was bleeding, he had a sprained knee and cuts on his feet. An ambulance took him to the hospital where his cuts were stitched up and he was treated for a concussion.

At the hospital Lance explained to his doctor that he was racing in a triathlon six days later. The doctor told him there was no way he would be ready. Lance disagreed. Before the race he took the brace off his knee, climbed on his bike and finished third. He later received a letter from the doctor who had treated him in the hospital.

"I can't believe it," the doctor wrote.

Trip to Russia

As a senior in high school, Lance qualified to train for the U.S. Olympic bicycling team in Colorado Springs, Colorado. As part of this training he also had the opportunity to go to Moscow, the capital of Russia, to race in the 1989 Junior World Championships. The only problem was his school, which said that the six weeks of classes both trips would cause him to miss was too much.

The school said that if Lance went, he would not be able to graduate with his class. Lance talked about this with his mother. They decided that the trip was important and he should go. She would figure out what to do about school.

In Moscow, Lance led the bike race for a few laps but did not pace himself well. Although he faded near the end of the race, he impressed everyone. The Russian coach said that Lance was the best cyclist he had seen in years.

When he got home, his mom had arranged for him to take courses at a private school for free. Although he graduated from the private school and not with his class as he had hoped, he was happy to have finished school on time.

Also during Lance's senior year, his mother married a man named John Walling. Lance and John got along well, and Lance was upset when John and his mother separated in 1998. Despite this disappointment, now that Lance had finished high school he was determined to focus all his energy on his main goal: becoming a professional cyclist.

3

LEARNING TO RACE

Lance remained in Plano during the summer of 1989. He hung around Jim Hoyt's bike store and began to race all over the United States for a team sponsored by Subaru-Montgomery. Racing in the U.S. was all right, but Lance knew the real bike-racing action was in Europe. Just as great baseball players in Japan want to play in the United States so they can compete against the best, Lance knew that he had to go to Europe if he wanted to prove he was the best cyclist in the world.

He got his chance early in 1990. The U.S. national cycling team had a new director named Chris Carmichael, a former Olympic cyclist who was looking for new kids to race for his team. Carmichael had heard about Lance, that he was a super-strong kid, but that he did not know much about how to race. He called Lance and asked him if he wanted to join the team and go to Europe. Lance did not have to think long before giving his answer.

The Bull of Texas

Lance's first big international race was the 1990 World Championships in Japan. It was a 115-mile race that included a steep, long hill climb. To make matters worse, the race was held on a hot summer day. Coach Carmichael told Lance to hold back during the race and save energy. He was not to make his move to the front until near the end of the race. But Lance did not follow instructions. He pushed to the front early in the race and ran out of energy before it was over. He dropped back to 11th place by the finish line.

His reputation as a strong kid who did not know how to race continued for a time. His first nickname in Europe was "Toro de Texas," the Bull of Texas, which was given to him by a Spanish reporter.

Lance made a promise to himself that he would stop racing like a bull. All his coaches had been right. Patient cyclists won races. Lance knew he had a lot to learn.

Back in the United States, Lance moved from Plano, a town he had never cared for, to Austin, Texas. He was much happier in Austin. Nobody cared what brand of jeans he wore, and the outskirts had plenty of back roads for him to train on.

Austin, Texas. (Austin Convention and Visitors Bureau)

Winning in Italy

Lance still raced for the Subaru-Montgomery team in the United States, and for the U.S. national team in Europe. In 1990 there was one race, in Italy, which both teams entered. It was called the Settimana Bergamasca, a 10-day race through the mountains of northern Italy. Lance rode for the U.S. team, so he was racing against Subaru-Montgomery. The trouble was, both of his coaches wanted to tell him what to do, and they were not telling him the same thing. His Subaru coach told him to support the other members of that team. Coach Carmichael, on the other

Chris Carmichael, former Olympic cyclist and one of Lance's first coaches. (Carmichael Training Systems)

hand, told him to attack and push for the lead. Lance knew which coach to listen to and he was soon out front.

It was then that he realized just how unpopular an American cyclist could be to European fans. The Italians who lined the course hated the fact that Lance was leading the race. Some of them even resorted to dirty tricks to make Lance lose. They threw thumbtacks and broken glass out in front of him, hoping they could give him a flat tire. But it didn't work and Lance won the race. Afterward, Carmichael proved to be a prophet of sorts: He told Lance that someday he was going to win the Tour de France.

Turning Pro

In 1991 Lance became the U.S. National Amateur Champion. He remained an amateur until 1992 so he could compete in the Olympics that year for the United

States. (Professionals were not allowed to participate in the Olympics at that time.) The Olympics were held in Barcelona, Spain, and he finished 14th in his event.

Following the Olympics, he turned pro. His performance in Barcelona was disappointing, but strong enough to impress Jim Ochowicz, the director of the Motorola pro team. Ochowicz offered Lance a contract. For Lance, Ochowicz would become more than a coach; he would become like the father Lance never knew.

Lance's first pro race was the Clásica San Sebastian in 1992. It was a single-day race, but more than 100 miles long. His introduction to pro racing was not a happy one. The race was held on one of the most miserable days of the year. An icy rain was pouring down. Lance's bones quickly grew cold, and then colder. He never wanted to drop out of a race so badly. To make matters worse, he kept slipping farther and farther behind. He finished dead-last, 27 minutes behind the winner. His pro career came close to ending that day, almost before it had begun. But his mother had taught him never to quit.

Lance did not have very long to feel sorry for himself. His next race was only two days away, the Championship of Zurich, in Switzerland. Lance did a lot better this time. It was not so much that he raced smarter than in the previous race. It was just that his last-place finish had embarrassed and angered him. He turned that anger into energy. He raced hard from the start and he never let down. He crossed the finish line second, and when he was done he knew he could make it as a professional cyclist.

But times were still tough. Lance was still not a patient racer. He still lost races that he knew he should have won. He would find himself thinking, "If I'm the strongest guy, why didn't I win?"

Being the Bad Guy

Lance knew that he was unpopular in Europe. At first he did nothing to change that. Part of him liked his "bad guy" image. The European press loved him because he would say whatever was on his mind, but his fellow racers began to dislike him and found ways to get back at him for his lack of respect. During races, other cyclists would move quickly into Lance's path, cutting him off, so that he had to slam on the brakes. Sometimes the others would push the pace when Lance wanted to hold back, making him work when he did not want to.

In the early days of Lance's pro racing career, one Italian racer purposefully finished fourth. He allowed others to pass him near the end of a race that Lance was winning, just so he would not have to stand on the winner's podium with Lance after the race.

During the European racing season, Lance lived in a rented apartment in Lake Como, Italy, which is in the

Alps. Living in Europe began to change Lance. He became more sophisticated. He dressed better. He learned to get along in several languages.

Lance has matured quite a bit since his early "bad boy" days in Europe. Although he is still unpopular with some European fans, he has learned to respect the other racers, and they have learned to respect him.

The Triple Crown

In 1993, Thrift Drugs sponsored a series of three races in the United States that was called the "Triple Crown of Cycling." If one racer won all three, he would win $1 million. The races were in Pittsburgh, West Virginia, and Philadelphia.

Lance was one of 120 cyclists trying to win the big cash prize. The Pittsburgh race took place over one day. The West Virginia race—the U.S. Pro Championships—was in stages and took place over six days. The third race was 156 miles through the streets of Philadelphia.

Lance won the first two races. After these victories he called his mom and told her to come to Philadelphia to cheer him on. For the third race, and possibly the biggest paycheck of his life, he was determined to race smartly. He thought about everything his coaches had ever told him. When the race started, he was patient. He hung back. He saved his energy. He did not make his move until there were only 20 miles left. Then he quickly pushed his way to the front and took the lead. With lots of energy left, he lengthened his lead and won by a large margin. He was greeted at the finish line by a swarm of reporters, but there was only one person he wanted to see: his mother. When he found her, they cried on each other's shoulders—exhausted, excited, and a million dollars richer.

Later that year he won one stage of the biggest bike race in the world, the Tour de France. It was the 114-mile stage from Châlons-sur-Marne to Verdun, and it happened during the event for which he would become most famous. Lance was only 21 years old. He was the youngest racer ever to win a Tour de France stage.

His success ran out at that point, however. By the 12th stage of the Tour he had slipped to 97th place, and soon thereafter he dropped out. Just as had been the case in his pro debut, the cold and rain had gotten to him.

Meeting a King

The 1993 World Championships were held in Oslo, Norway. Lance again invited his mom to come watch the race. After all, she had been his good luck charm in Philadelphia. She arrived a few days early while Lance psyched himself up for the race.

Things did not look good on the morning of the event. The rain was coming down in sheets and the forecast said that weather would hold throughout the day. This rain made the race very difficult, and not just because it soaked the racers and made it impossible for them to stay warm. It also soaked the roads, mixed with the oil and gas that had been spilled by cars, and made the course extremely slippery. Racers were wiping out all over the place.

Lance fell twice during the race but both times was able to get back on his bike and under way before losing too much ground. He once again was determined to race smart. He hung back with the pack until late in the race, when he pushed for the front on an uphill stretch. He gained the lead and kept pushing. By the time he looked back to see how much of a lead he had, he couldn't even see the second-place cyclist. He won the race and once again got a tearful hug from his mom at the finish line.

Soon after winning he learned that the king of Norway, King Harald, wanted to meet him. He and his mom went to the palace. When the guard told him that the king wanted to see him alone Lance said, "I don't check my mother at the door." After a few moments, King Harald agreed to meet with them both.

Just as had been the case with his stage-win at the Tour de France, he was the youngest all-time winner of the World Championships.

The 1993 racing season was a very good one for Lance. He won 10 titles in all.

4

THE TOUR

By 1994, the cycling world had noticed Lance. Because bicycle racing is so much more popular in Europe than it is in the United States, he became famous across the Atlantic first. He had even started to make friends in the European racing community. One of these friends was the Belgian cyclist Eddy Merckx, one of the few men to have won the Tour de France five times.

Merckx was a legend in the sport. He took Lance under his wing and gave him advice. He said that Lance had the mental and physical strength to win the Tour de France, but that he would have to lose weight. Lance at that time had a heavily muscled body. He was built more like a football player than a cyclist. It is an advantage for a cyclist to be light because this decreases the amount of weight he has to carry up those long uphill stretches. The trick was to lose weight without losing strength. The key, Lance learned, was in diet. He would have to eat less but still get just as much nutrition. Although that meant giving up some of his favorites, like cheeseburgers and Tex-Mex food, he was willing to make the sacrifice in order to reach his goal.

The Super Bowl of Bicycle Races

The Tour de France is the Super Bowl of bicycle races. It is the biggest race of the year. It has been called the world's largest sporting event. During the event the racers take a tour of the entire country, just as the name implies. About 200 cyclists ride in the Tour de France every year.

Lance and Eddie Merckx, 2002. (Reuters New Media Inc./ CORBIS)

The 2,000-mile course changes from year to year, but it usually goes all around the outside of the country, and it always ends in Paris. Each year, hundreds of towns ask to be part of the route, paying good money to do so. To make the race even more intense, the Tour is held in the summer when the weather is at its hottest.

The Tour started in 1903. It was the idea of a sportswriter for the French newspaper *L'Auto*. Sixty cyclists raced in the first Tour. Twenty-one of them finished. It was popular right from the start. About 100,000 spectators came out to stand along the route during the first race, and the crowds have been getting a little bit bigger every year since. For the first seven years, the racecourse was pretty much flat. In 1910, the race became even more difficult, as the racers now had to ride up and down treacherous mountains.

Over the years, the race has taken place in some difficult circumstances. In 1914, World War I started during the Tour. The race finished as the route for some of the early stages turned into a battlefield. The race was not held from 1915 to 1918 because of World War I and was canceled again from 1940 until 1946 because of World War II.

A Fierce Competition

The race takes place over three weeks and four weekends. The cyclists race from one point to another in a series of daylong races called stages. The rules of the International Cycling Union say that there must be two days of rest during the Tour, and the average daily stage cannot be longer than 120 miles.

Each racer is timed on a clock. The cyclist who finishes all of the stages in the least total time wins the race. A racer can win many stages and still not win the race, if he has one very bad day. On the other hand, a racer can win the Tour de France without winning a single stage. This happened in both 1956 and 1966.

After each stage the times are added up and the racer who is in the lead gets to wear a yellow jersey for the next stage. This helps the thousands of spectators know when the leader passes by.

There are other honorary jerseys as well. The race's best sprinter—that is, the racer who can go short distances the fastest—wears a green jersey. The best climber, the racer who goes the fastest uphill over the course of the race, wears a polka-dotted jersey. The best young rider, the leader among those who are 25 years old or younger, wears a white jersey.

What if a racer is leading in more than one category? What if the racer is the leader of the race, under 25 years old, and is the best at going up the sides of mountains? To keep riders from having to wear layers of colorful jerseys, there is a pecking order. The yellow jersey is most important, followed by the green, polka dot, and white. The racer wears the most important jersey for which he qualifies. Rather than have no one wear the other jerseys, the second-place racer in each category gets to wear it. Each jersey is worn during each stage, even if the same racer leads in all categories.

History tells us that it is easy to predict who will wear the green jersey. The same racers tend to be the best sprinters year after year. But the best climber is often a surprise. Unknown but gutsy cyclists sometimes find themselves wearing polka dots. Whereas the sprinting jersey is won with talent, the climbing jersey requires courage, as well.

A Team Effort

Although single racers win the race and individuals wear the jerseys, the Tour de France is made up of teams of racers. Each team has nine racers who share a single sponsor. The sponsor pays all of its racers' bills in exchange for publicity. So the racers do everything they can to get their sponsor's name in the newspapers and on TV as much as possible. Racers mention their sponsor every time they are interviewed, and they wear their sponsor's name on their clothes and bicycle.

The teams of racers will sometimes race as a team, blocking the wind for their best racer when he needs a breather. (It takes 30 percent less energy to go uphill behind other cyclists than it does with the wind in your face.) Or the team will send out "rabbits," racers who will lead the pack and wear out competition by setting a too-fast pace. The idea is always to get one of the jerseys on a teammate's back. That way the sponsor gets more publicity.

If a team does not have a racer with a real chance of winning the Tour, they may exhaust themselves early in an attempt to win one or more stages. Because of this, the winners of the Tour's early stages are rarely the winner of the Tour. The winner of the Tour usually does not win any of the early stages. That cyclist is usually playing it smart and saving energy for the tough days to come. Because of this, the pace of early stages is fastest and slows down steadily as the Tour goes along.

Although there are only nine racers on each team, the team may employ more than 20 people. There are mechanics on hand to repair the bikes if one breaks from wear or during an accident. There are press-relations people who make sure that their team members and sponsors, of course, receive good coverage in the media. The teams also employ *soigneurs*, or caregivers. They are like road managers who provide basics such as food, lodging, and basic first-aid for the team members. That way the racers only have to worry about the race.

A car filled with the team's support staff rides in a car behind the *peloton*, the French term for the pack of cyclists who tend to move together during a stage. Everything a racer could possibly need is in that car. There are even backup bikes for each cyclist piled on top of the car in case a bike breaks so badly that no quick repair is possible.

The teams' leaders (called directors, but who function more like head coaches) have walkie-talkie devices so they can give instructions to each cyclist. Each rider is also wired up to a heart monitor, so a staff member back in the car can tell just how fast everyone's heart is beating. In this way, the director will know if any cyclist is working harder than he should.

Although the racers enjoy plenty of rest and a controlled diet when they are not racing, during the race it is a different story. The snacks and drinks are sugary and designed to give them a quick boost of energy. Energizing athletic drinks replenish all of the sweat the cyclists lose, and different types of cookies are the snack of choice.

Like many sports, cycling is a sport that calls for good manners. The Tour fans may be rude to the racers sometimes, but the cyclists have strict rules of politeness for each other. If a train crosses the race path, those that have passed the tracks will stop and wait for those whose path is blocked. Of course, those who break the rules are often paid back in the unkindest manner.

Unfortunately, the Tour has always had a reputation for some underhanded behavior. Cheating started soon after the Tour became an annual event. For example, at times, members of one team have slipped drugs into the drinks of the competition. Or the cyclist leading the pack has tossed thumbtacks onto the road behind him so that those following him would get a flat tire. Race officials do their best to prevent such activities, which are thankfully rare, but the fierce competition can bring out the best and the worst in some athletes.

Lance raced for an American team called Team Motorola, named after its sponsor. This team was different from most of the American teams that had competed in the Tour. Not only were they good, they had a chance to win. For the first time in the history of the sport, an American team—Lance's team—was ranked among the top five in the world.

Ready to Go for It

Through 1994 Lance had never finished a Tour de France. Many coaches do not allow their young racers to complete the race until they are ready. They start out racing in just a few stages, and the following year they race a few more.

That is why in 1993 Lance had won a stage of the Tour but did not complete the entire race. In 1995 he was ready to go for it.

At 23, Lance was still very young for a long-distance racer. He had built a reputation as the winner of one-day races, but as someone who struggled in stage races. By 1995 he was eager to erase that from his résumé. He was determined to finish the 1995 Tour, and though he accomplished this goal, the race is not a happy memory for Lance.

Tragedy

Tragedy marred the 1995 Tour and reminded everyone of just how dangerous the sport can be. Armstrong's teammate and friend Fabio Casartelli was killed during a high-speed downhill stretch. He fell off his bike and struck the back of his head and neck on a curb. As Lance rode by the accident he could see that several riders had fallen and that a group of concerned onlookers had gathered around one of them, but he did not learn until later what had happened.

Later in the day Lance was told by team radio that Fabio was dead. At the end of the stage the team had a meeting to decide what to do. Some of them, including Lance, wanted to drop out of the race. Others wanted to continue, as a tribute to Fabio. It was decided the team would

Fabio Casartelli, Lance's friend and teammate, was involved in a fatal accident during the 1995 Tour de France. (Associated Press)

stay in the race. There was no racing the following day. The *peloton* stayed together and rode in formation, like a funeral procession, as a tribute to Fabio, and Lance's team was allowed to win the stage. The next day, the 18th stage of the Tour, it was back to racing as usual. It was to be Lance's day.

Armstrong won the stage. In fact, he won it going away. He had forgotten all about the smart way to race. He had pushed to the front way too early, but he did not run out

Lance, finishing a stage of the 1995 Tour de France, holds up his hands in tribute to Fabio Casartelli. (Graham Watson)

of gas. He was still going strong at the finish. There was more than a minute at the end between Lance and the second-place finisher.

He later wrote: "I didn't feel a moment's pain. Instead I felt something spiritual. I know that I rode with a higher purpose that day. Even though I had charged too early, I never suffered after I broke away. I would like to think that was Fabio's experience too. He simply broke away and separated from the world. There is no doubt in my mind that there were two riders on that bike. Fabio was with me."

5

CANCER

Things were going great for Lance during the first months of 1996. That year he signed a contract to race for the French team Cofidis for $2.5 million. He had bought a new house—a big house. And he had recently bought his own powerboat and Jet Ski.

Then he began to feel sick. At first he tried to ignore it. Living with pain is what cyclists do. They live in a painful world. The guy who can take the most pain usually wins the race.

When Lance's right testicle became swollen, he tried not to think about it. He figured he had hurt himself on his bike. But the pain and the swelling got worse.

Then came that year's Tour de France and another sign that something was seriously wrong. Thinking that he had a bad chest cold, Lance dropped out of the race after only five days. He told the press that he couldn't get back on his bike because he could not breathe.

The next sign that Lance was seriously ill came at a party. He was having a great time hanging out with his friends, when he suddenly came down with a bad headache. It was the worst headache he had ever had. At first he thought it was caused by the alcohol he had consumed. But the headache got worse. He took a couple types of medicine his friends had given him. Nothing worked.

Then one morning he coughed up blood—a lot of blood. Scared, he talked to a friend about it. The friend said that he probably had a sinus infection. That would explain the headache as well. Lance wanted to believe him, but he suspected something more serious was wrong. He was tired all the time, and he slept more than he ever had before.

The swelling in his testicle became much worse, and he could no longer sit on his bike at all. He had to ride standing up for an entire training session. Finally, Lance asked a friend to call a doctor for him.

The doctor who first looked at Lance sent him right away for X rays. Before the day was out, Lance knew what was wrong.

Cancer.

He had cancer in his testicle and in his lungs. Lance did not want to believe it but deep down inside he knew it was true. It explained why he could not sit down on his bike and why he was coughing up blood. Surgery to remove his testicle was scheduled for the next day, as his cancer was spreading.

Leaving the doctor's office, Lance faced the tough task of telling his friends and his girlfriend at the time that his racing career and possibly his life were over. He managed to do this, but he couldn't bring himself to tell his mom. His friend Rick Parker told her for him.

Surgery and Therapy

The day after the doctors found the cancer, Lance's infected testicle was removed. A few days later he began a form of treatment called chemotherapy, or "chemo." He had chemicals pumped into him that would kill the cancer in his body. Unfortunately, as it does in most patients, chemotherapy also made his hair fall out and made him feel very sick. The chemicals used are so strong that patients cannot take them every day. They take it in three-week cycles. After two weeks of chemo a patient takes a week off so his or her body can recover. The trick is to poison the cancer without poisoning the entire body.

No matter how sick Lance became, he never stopped exercising. After his operation, when he was unable to ride his bike, he would still put on his sweat suit and headphones and go for long walks. He would also walk a new route to see things he had never seen before. As soon as he could ride his bike he did, and again he always sought out new roads, never repeating previous journeys.

Another Race

In Lance's brain, beating cancer became another race that he had to train for. Because of the effects of chemo he did not want to eat, but he forced himself. Without eating he would not have energy and without energy he would not be able to ride. If he could not ride, he would die. So he ate.

He discovered he had no health insurance that would cover his medical treatments. He had to sell his sports car to help pay the bills.

Lance decided that if he was going to defeat cancer, he was going to have to know his enemy. He went to bookstores and bought every book he could find about cancer. He became an expert in the subject. He had never been much of a reader before, but now he always had his nose in a book, even medical journals.

Only a week after he learned he had cancer, Lance received more bad news. His condition was even worse than doctors had first thought. The cancer had spread into his brain. That was what had caused the serious headache. Doctors who at first said Lance's chances of surviving were fifty-fifty were no longer so confident.

His chances were now, they said, one in five. Even that was an optimistic estimate.

Choosing a Treatment

Around this time Lance first learned how popular he was. He began to receive great stacks of "get well" mail. Much of it came from fans, but some from doctors who had suggestions.

One letter came from Dr. Steven Wolff, a fan of Lance's who was also a surgeon at the Vanderbilt University medical center. He urged Lance to look into possible treatments he could receive in Indiana, Houston, and New York. Lance looked into them all. He finally decided that he liked the doctors and the attitude best in Indiana. While the doctors in Houston and New York thought they might be able to cure him, they said their treatments would hurt his lungs. He would not be able to race on his bike again.

The doctors in Indiana were different. They not only thought they could cure Lance, but they could do it without harming his lungs. They told him he would live to race again.

While trying to decide where he would receive his treatment, Lance began to talk to his cancer as if it were a person. He told it that he was going to kick its butt. He told it that it had picked the wrong fellow when it decided to attack him.

He would need an operation on his brain to remove the cancer there. The brain surgeon, Dr. Scott Shapiro, told him that he was lucky. The tumors were on the outside of his brain, and they were easier to get to that way. The surgeon could just scrape them off, rather than cut into the brain to get to them.

Many of his friends made the trip with him to Indiana. Lance checked into the hospital and had his head shaved. Colored dots were placed on his scalp indicating where the tumors were. The doctor needed to know where to cut through Lance's scalp and skull.

The night before his surgery Lance was as scared as he had ever been, afraid that he would die on the operating

Indiana University Hospital and Outpatient Center, where Lance underwent surgery and treatment for cancer.
(Courtesy of Clarian Health Partners)

table. His surgeon told him this was normal. To be unafraid of brain surgery would not be normal. Then the surgeon assured Lance that he was the best brain surgeon in the world.

Doctors operated on Lance's brain on October 25, 1996. Before the operation, nurses gave Lance three words to remember. They were "ball, pin, driveway." After the operation they would ask him to repeat the words. This was to check if the operation had done any damage to Lance's brain.

A drug was used to put Lance to sleep during his operation. He was out for about six hours. The cancer cells were removed from his brain. When Lance woke up he said, "ball, pin, driveway," to prove that he still had his memory. Dr. Shapiro told him that the operation had gone even better than expected.

Lance was moved from the recovery area outside the operating room to a section of the hospital called intensive care, where the very sickest patients are treated. Looking in the mirror, Lance could see that his head was completely wrapped in bandages. He told a nurse that he was hungry and she fed him scrambled eggs. His mother sat at his bedside and held his hand.

After a while his friends, with frightened looks on their faces, came in groups of twos and threes to see him. He stayed in intensive care until the next morning, when he was moved to another room.

He had to begin his chemo treatments right away. There were still the tumors in his lungs to worry about and any other cancer cells the doctors may not have found. Only 24 hours after his surgery, Lance decided that he wanted to go out to dinner. It was a little too soon, however. Before dinner was through, Lance started to feel ill and asked to return to the hospital. He stayed in the hospital for six days after his operation.

In addition to his health, Lance had other worries as well. He still did not have any health insurance, and it is often very difficult to get this insurance after one is seriously ill. One of Lance's sponsors, Oakley, makers of cycling accessories, went to bat for him. They threatened their insurance carrier that they would move all of their insurance business to another company if the carrier did not cover Lance's bills. The insurance company did not like the deal, but they agreed to do it.

Four Cycles

Lance was happy that he had come through the operation so well, but his happiness did not last. It was not long before the chemo treatments were making him feel very, very sick.

After his cancer surgery, Lance struggled to regain his energy and health so that he could ride once again. He succeeded. (www.cycleofhope.org)

He constantly felt as if he were being poisoned. When he could sleep, he did. When he could not sleep, he often could not do anything except stare at the wall. The chemo treatments went through four cycles that lasted a total of three months.

So Lance felt sick for the rest of that year. His last treatment came on December 13. During each cycle, the doctors would allow the poisons to build up in his body until they were just about to kill him. Then he would be allowed a break to flush out the chemo. When his body was again clean, they would start with the treatments again. The chemo treatments, after all, killed more than just the cancer cells. They killed healthy cells as well.

The treatments made Lance feel sick to his stomach all the time. Eating was not easy. He found that the only thing he could eat and keep down were apple fritters from the hospital cafeteria. All of his hair fell out and his skin turned gray.

"I think I'm supposed to live."

Lance's mother stayed with him as much as she could. But her vacation days soon ran out and she had to go back to work. Jim Ochowicz, Lance's coach and friend, took his mom's place and sat by Lance's side while he received each chemo treatment intravenously. During one session

Lance told Jim, "Och, I don't feel ready to go. I think I'm supposed to live."

During Lance's time in the hospital he began to believe in angels—angels in human form. These included the nurses who took care of him. His favorite was a nurse named LaTrice. She once said to him: "I hope someday to be just a figment of your imagination. After you leave here, I hope I never see you ever again." After giving it some thought, Lance realized it was the nicest thing anyone had ever said to him.

Lance saved his anger for his cancer. He still talked to his cancer, but not on friendly terms. He even had a nickname for his cancer, which cannot be repeated here.

Although Oakley had pledged its full support to Lance during his illness, not all of Lance's sponsors felt that way. Cofidis, who had signed Lance to a $2.5 million contract to race for their team, began to worry that they were not going to get their money's worth out of him. They sent a representative to see Lance, who looked very bad at the time. The French company decided that Lance was going to die. Cofidis ended up paying Lance less than a third of what they had agreed to.

Between chemo cycles Lance returned to Texas and tried to exercise as much as he could by riding his bike or going for walks. His doctors told him that staying in shape was the last of his worries and that he should not put his body under additional stress. But Lance did not listen. He continued to go out on his bike. He rode even though embarrassing and frightening things happened. A woman in her 50s riding a heavy cross-country bike passed him on a hill, and, on another ride, he lost his breath so badly the friends who were with him wanted to call an ambulance. He refused the ride, waited until he had caught his breath, and rode back home. The bike rides did not stop.

Lance had 14 tumors in all. He still carries the scars of his cancer surgery. Most noticeable are the two scars on his head from his brain surgery. Each is six inches long. They are a quarter-inch deep and shaped like horseshoes.

Through intense treatment and his own determination, Lance survived his bout with cancer. Today he is an inspiration to cancer patients and their families everywhere. Although his situation looked hopeless, he survived. His name serves as a beacon of hope in hospitals around the world.

And he has learned to live for the moment.

"Before cancer," he told one reporter, "I was always worrying about what I was going to be doing five or six years down the road. It's a terrible way to live. When I was the sickest, I decided, I'm never going to waste another today thinking about tomorrow. This is it. Today is all I have."

Since his cure, he goes on motocross rides in Mexico, he has learned how to surf, he owns a sports car, and he loves to drive fast. Even cancer could not kill Lance's life-long love of speed.

The Obligation of the Cured

Once cured, Lance felt what is called the "obligation of the cured." That is, it was now his job to inspire other people with cancer and to help them get well. It is a job that he will take on for the rest of his life.

The Lance Armstrong Foundation and Cycle of Hope (a partnership between LAF and Bristol-Myers Squibb) encourage research, support, fund-raising, and education for the benefit of cancer survivors, their loved ones, and the general public. (www.cycleofhope.org)

Even before he had been given his clear bill of health, he began to visit cancer patients, mostly children, to tell them how important it is to fight the illness. He started the Lance Armstrong Foundation, which helps raise money to battle the disease. Each year the organization sponsors Ride for the Roses, a bike race to raise money.

Just because tests showed that Lance's body was cancer-free did not mean that he could relax. It could always come back, and if it did, it would probably kill him. Doctors said that if his cancer did return, it was most apt to do so in the first year. That was a very long year. Doctors had to check him frequently, and each time he had to wait for the results, fearing the worst. But each checkup brought the same news, and it was the best news he could hear. He was cancer-free and staying that way.

And the Indiana doctors had kept their promise. They had killed his cancer without harming his lungs. His body was intact.

6

COMEBACK

Along with a new drive to live every minute of his life to the fullest, Lance's period of illness gave him something else: his wife, Kristin. He met her one month after his last chemo treatment, in January 1997. Kristin Richard, who everyone called Kik (pronounced *keek*), worked for one of the sponsors of Ride for the Roses. Lance thought she was smart and pretty, but at first they did not get along. Their first real conversation turned into a fight, but things got better after that. Lance invited Kik to attend the weekly meetings of his cancer foundation, to think up new ways to raise money and inspire patients.

She says, "I got to know Lance when he was standing on the edge between life and death. It was awesome to be part of. I felt like he showed me the view from that cliff. That bonds two people. And if you get to come back down from that edge, it changes your life. You never want to miss out on anything fun or beautiful or scary again."

The first Ride for the Roses raised $200,000. The donation Lance remembers best is the $5,000 he got from Jim Hoyt, Lance's old friend and mentor, who sold him his first bike.

In the meantime Lance broke up with his old girlfriend, and his feelings toward Kik were warming up. They began to do everything together and soon were in love.

Golf Every Day

In 1997 Armstrong returned to his bicycle and began to train. But all did not go smoothly. There were reasons to start racing again soon. For one thing, that was how Lance made money. But Lance's body was still telling him to take it easy—something his body had never said to him before he got sick. He started training four hours a day, but afterward he would feel completely worn out. He caught colds frequently.

Of course, each time he felt ill, he feared the worst, that his cancer had returned. But it was always just a cold. Because of what his body had been through, he could not fight them off the way he used to. His immune system needed a chance to recharge itself, like a battery. He could tell that he was not going to be able to race seriously in 1997, and he feared that he might never be able to again.

He began to tell his friends that he was retired. He was an ex-cyclist. He ate fast food and played golf every day.

The U.S. Postal Service team in the Tour de France. (Getty Images)

That year Kik went to Spain on vacation and Lance went along. It was the first time he had been to Europe for anything other than racing or training. They went to Monaco,

and then to France where Lance had to tend to some business. He talked to reporters and met with his sponsors. By the time they returned Lance's hair had returned and he once again looked like a healthy man.

The U.S. Postal Service

Lance felt stronger every day, but he had grown lazy. He began to feel as if he were wasting his life. He made up his mind that he was going to race again. He announced his comeback at a press conference on September 4, 1997. He had expected offers from sponsors and racing teams to come rolling in, but they didn't. Racing experts, he found, had given up on him.

Then came an offer. The U.S. Postal Service was forming a racing team. It was to be completely funded and sponsored by U.S. money. Lance knew the man who was putting the team together. He was San Francisco millionaire Thomas Weisel, who had once owned the Subaru-Montgomery team that Lance had raced for. The new U.S. Postal team made Lance an interesting offer. They said they would pay him a low salary, but he would get bonus money depending on how well he did. If Lance's comeback was successful, he could make a lot of money.

Lance signed a contract in October. The news was announced at a press conference in San Francisco. He told the reporters that he saw no reason why he could not become as good of a racer as ever. He was out of shape from not racing, but he planned to get back into shape quickly. He said he would spend the rest of the year in the United States training and then would travel to Europe to race for the first time in a year and half.

After returning to Texas, Lance and his mother went shopping for an engagement ring. Soon after that, following a romantic dinner for two, Lance proposed to Kik and she accepted.

Troubled Sleep

Training camp for the Postal team was in Santa Barbara, California, and lasted for two months. Lance surprised everyone with how quickly he got back into shape. His body responded well to the training, but his mind got back into racing shape more slowly. The one-year anniversary of the discovery of his cancer had come and gone. The chances the disease would return were now slim. But he still couldn't get the fear out of his mind. His sleep was troubled by nightmares.

Lance and Kik moved to France in January 1998. Kik gave up her job and her dog to make the move. She concentrated on learning French so it would be easier for her to communicate.

Lance, in the meantime, was having a tough time with his comeback. He had forgotten just how much cyclists have to suffer. He had forgotten about the bad hotels and grueling schedules. Perhaps there was a part of him that felt that he had been through and suffered enough. The last time he was in Europe, it had been on vacation with Kik. Everything had been nice—luxurious even. Now it was time to suffer and work again. He was not sure he was ready.

Business was not going well, either. Lance's agent Bill Stapleton was having trouble getting new sponsors for Lance. Lance began to take out his frustrations on Bill, who was so upset that he quit—temporarily, at least.

The first race of Lance's comeback was the five-day Ruta del Sol in Spain. He finished 14th, which everyone except Lance considered good. Reporters only wanted to talk to him about his cancer. It was driving him crazy.

After a two-week break, Lance competed in his second race, the eight-day Paris-to-Nice race. It was held in icy-cold, windy, wet weather. In the Prologue, the time trial to determine who would get to ride at the front of the *peloton*, Lance finished 19th. This was very frustrating for Lance, since he was used to doing much better. During that race, with weather that was just as bad as predicted, he quit. He told Kik that he did not know how much time he had left to live, and he did not feel like spending his remaining days suffering on a bicycle. She said that whatever he wanted was okay with her.

Lance's friends sensed that it was Lance's emotions rather than his common sense that were making his decisions for him. They told him that he should wait a little while before he announced to the world that he was never going to race again.

His agent told him that he would be helping out his charity if he did not announce his retirement until after the Ride for the Roses in May. Lance agreed to put off the announcement and told himself he was going to take a few days off to think.

A "Bum and a Slob"

Those few days turned into months. Some days he would-n't shave—or bother to get dressed. His only activity was playing golf, which he did every day. Kik remained patient for a while, but finally she told him that it was about time he made up his mind. Was he going to do something with the rest of his life, or was he content to be, as she said, a "bum and a slob"?

Lance faced some challenges to his comeback in 1998, including a lack of sponsors and some disappointing races. But he bounced back with some encouragement from family and friends. (www.cycleofhope.org)

Finally, Kik and Lance's coaches and his agent got together and successfully convinced him to race one more time. It was the U.S. Pro Championships in June and Lance agreed. He got back on his bike for good in April.

To train he went to Boone, North Carolina, a place for which he had happy memories. He liked the people—"hippies," he called them—and twice he had won races there. Lance had a lot of work to do. He had again grown fat and out of shape. He rented a cabin and went to work.

This time the hard work agreed with both his body and his brain. He worked hard, and felt great. He ate only the correct foods and got back into shape faster than would seem humanly possible.

One day, when he rode for six hours and then left his training partners in the dust going up the side of Beech Mountain, he knew that he was back. He was not just ready to race again—he was ready to win.

Wedding Day

On May 8, 1998, Lance married Kristin in Santa Barbara, California. By this time, Lance was back to riding his bike every day, so naturally he rode his bike to the ceremony. About 100 friends and relatives attended the ceremony and the party afterward.

Lance and Kik honeymooned in a nearby beach house, but even that did not stop Lance's training. He rode many hours every day. Kik was going to have to get used to being second to Lance's bike.

Lance returned to Austin, Texas, in May to ride in his own event, the Ride for the Roses. He won the race, which thrilled Kik to no end. It was his first win since they had met.

In June he went to Philadelphia for the U.S. Pro Championships. This was the "one race" he had promised to ride in before retiring. But, by this time, he had forgotten all about retirement. He finished fourth in Philadelphia.

Back to Europe

After the race, he told Kik it was time for them to go back to Europe. Lance and Kik rented an apartment in France. She once again began to take French lessons, and Lance rejoined the U.S. Postal team. His first race after returning was the four-day Tour of Luxembourg and he won. Next stop was the Netherlands for the seven-day Tour of Holland, where he finished fourth.

Lance decided that he still was not ready for the grueling Tour de France, the biggest race of all. There simply was not enough time for him to prepare properly, so he sat it out in 1998. Instead, he got a job doing TV commentary.

That year's Tour turned out to be an ugly event. French police raided the cars of the racing teams and found steroids, which are illegal drugs used to help racers go faster for longer distances. Cyclists and race officials were put in jail.

Only two-thirds of the teams who started the race finished it. Some of the teams did not finish because they were behind bars. Others were out of the race because they had quit in protest.

Lance rejoined the racing tour after the Tour de France. With his future once again looking bright, he and Kik bought a house in France. His next race was his toughest test yet, the 23-day, 2,348-mile Tour of Spain. He suffered through the wind and the rain to finish fourth, only two minutes and 18 seconds behind the winner. It was the closest he had ever come to winning a race of that length. If he could come that close to winning the Tour of Spain, he knew he could win the Tour de France.

Good News

Because of Lance's operation and cancer treatments, he and Kik knew that having children might be difficult. So it was especially exciting when they learned in February 1999 that Kik was going to have a baby.

Although the 1999 racing season will be remembered as a very good one for Lance, it got off to a bad start. He crashed in the second race of the year and injured his shoulder. It was not broken, but he needed two weeks off to let it heal.

Lance crashed again in his first race back. A French woman appeared to swerve her car off the road to hit Lance. He was shaken up but not injured. In the next race he hit an oily spot on the road during a rainstorm and fell off his bike.

It was time to regroup. He took some time off and worked on racing fundamentals. As a young racer he had been good at the short races but struggled on the long ones. He had been prone to using up his energy too early in a race and having nothing left for the finish. Now, as he matured, he found that the exact opposite was true. He struggled in the one-day races. He realized why this was true. His body and his mind were now geared toward winning the Tour de France. In fact, winning the Tour de France and becoming a father were the only things he thought about.

The director of the U.S. Postal Team was Johan Bruyeel, an experienced Tour de France cyclist. Bruyeel has twice won stages of the Tour, in 1993 and 1995. Just as a baseball team has spring-training camp before the start of a season, Bruyeel took his team to the French mountain range called the Pyrenees to prepare for the Tour. Lance's attitude toward mountains, as it had been in the past, was, "Bring 'em on!"

Since Lance could not train 24 hours a day, he spent his time off his bike turning the Tour de France into a math problem. He used a computer to figure out his body's ideal weight, the best way for that weight to be distributed, and the best ratio of his weight to his bike's weight.

When he ate, each portion of food was carefully weighed so that he was getting precisely the correct nutrition. For breakfast, before his training began, he ate muesli breakfast cereal, fruit, and bread. If an extra-grueling day was planned, he would have scrambled egg whites. He was on his bike straight through till midafternoon. He took a nap and then had dinner—usually a weighed portion of macaroni.

Lance had lost a lot of weight during his cancer treatments. Much of it he never put back on once he regained his health. His racing weight was down 15 pounds from what it had been before he got sick. That was 15 pounds less he had to haul up the sides of mountains on his bike.

A Team of Two

When it came to preparing for the Tour, being married gave Lance an advantage over his teammates. Kik cooked and cleaned. When he trained in the mountains, she delivered his food to him. Lance only had to worry about the upcoming race.

Lance's first race of the 1999 season was the one-day Amstel Gold Race in April. It turned into a two-man race

The Tour de France course is full of winding roads and hilly terrain. (Getty Images)

between Lance and Michael Boogerd of the Netherlands, with Boogerd winning by inches after a sprint to the finish.

As the Tour de France grew nearer Lance's training sessions became tougher. He began to climb three mountains a day. The hardest mountain to climb near Lance's home was the Col de la Madone. Many cyclists would climb it once or twice a year as part of their training. Lance climbed it once a month, until he could climb it faster than any cyclist ever. The old record was 31 minutes, 30 seconds. Lance broke that record by 43 seconds. Lance knew that he had a serious chance to win the Tour de France. Cycling experts still had their doubts.

Lance got his share of publicity in Europe, because he was coming back to the sport after being sick, but the European press did not see him and the U.S. Postal Service team as serious contenders.

Kik and Lance went to Paris at the beginning of July for the pre-Tour activities. Like all of the other racers, Lance had to take a blood test to make sure he wasn't taking illegal drugs. He was given a guidebook that mapped out the entire course.

Donning the Yellow Jersey

The first stage of the Tour, as always, was the Prologue, the time trial to see who would get to ride at the front of the *peloton*. The Prologue was a sprint about six miles long. It was held that year in a small town called Le Puy du Fou. The cyclists race the Prologue one at a time against a clock. The one with the best time wins. Lance finished the course with the fastest time: eight minutes and two seconds. For the first time in his life he was the leader in the Tour de France. He went to the top of the podium where he was presented with the yellow jersey.

The next few stages of the race were across a flat section of northern France. Lance gave up his lead. He knew that there would be plenty of time to catch up when they got to the mountains. His job during these early stages was to be careful and avoid disaster.

Just such a disaster occurred during the second stage. Luckily for him, it happened behind Lance and he was not involved. It was rainy and the roads were slippery. One racer crashed and many others plowed into him, causing a huge pile of fallen cyclists and bikes. Two of Lance's toughest competitors, Alex Zuille and Michael Boogerd, were caught up in the crash and fell several minutes behind.

Lance rode a smart race, not burning up too much energy in stages he knew he would not win anyway.

The Race of Truth

After a few stages across flat land there was a second time trial. Unlike the Prologue, which was a short sprint, this one was about 40 miles long and was designed to determine the strongest racers. The second time trial, which began in the town of Metz, was known as the "Race of Truth." Not only was it long, but there also were two long uphill stretches.

Lance started out racing hard, perhaps a little too hard. He did not run out of gas and limp home, but he did have to fight the pain to finish strong. Just as had been the case in the Prologue, Lance's time was the fastest in the field. He was once again the overall leader, and he put the yellow jersey back on.

Into the Mountains

Then it was into the Alps mountain range, the part of the race where Lance knew he had trained harder than everyone else. Lance had a better than two-minute lead, but it was the sort of advantage that could disappear quickly in the mountains.

Lance's teammates helped him in every way they could. Since it is easier to pull away from the pack when riding alone, Lance's teammates never let the racers who were trying to catch Lance get by themselves. When one contender would break away from the pack, a U.S. Postal racer would follow and stay as close to him as possible. The racer in front would have to "pull" the one behind, forcing him to slow down. On the other hand, the other U.S. Postal cyclists would ride right in front of Lance, so he was being pulled and climbing the sides of mountains was that much easier.

With six miles left to go in the stage, Lance was 32 seconds behind the stage leader. But the leader was getting tired, and Lance felt like he had a lot of energy left to burn.

The team strategy had worked, and, for Lance, so had all of that hard training. He began to race harder and quickly made up time. He passed the stage leader and left him in the dust. Not only wasn't he going to lose his overall lead, he was going to lengthen it.

In the next stage he only finished fifth, but those who were immediately behind him for the overall lead did even worse. His overall lead continued to grow. By the time the Tour left the Alps, Lance's lead was almost eight minutes long.

Dirty Rumors

It was at this point that the French press began to say nasty things about Lance. They wrote that it was impossible for an American cyclist to handle the Tour de France as easily as Lance was doing. He had to be cheating. He had to be taking illegal drugs, they said.

Then came the five stages through central France between the two mountain ranges. These are called "transition stages." They are not flat, but rather hilly. The weather became very hot during these days, making life that much tougher for the cyclists. It was so hot that the pavement on the roads was softening, which also made for tougher riding conditions.

Being so far in the lead, Lance was now a marked man when it came to the other cyclists. Everyone was out to get Lance and his teammates. Other teams got together and made Lance work as hard as possible. But Lance and his teammates handled every situation.

As the race approached the second mountain range, the Pyrenees, the stories in the newspapers claiming that Lance was cheating got even worse. Lance started to become angry. At first he tried to ignore the stories, but he began to answer reporters' questions.

"I can emphatically say I am not on drugs," he said. "I thought a rider with my history and my health situation wouldn't be such a surprise. I'm not a new rider. I know there's been looking, and prying, and digging, but you're not going to find anything. There's nothing to find."

He told the members of the press that they should act like professionals and realize that the things they were printing simply were not true.

On the first stage in the Pyrenees, Lance had a tough time of it. The stage traveled up, down, and around seven mountains. There was no time to relax. Many of the roads were along the edge of cliffs. Any cyclist who rode off the road could plummet to his death.

It was another very hot day. Lance did okay until the last climb of the day when he ran out of energy. He managed to finish, but his lead was cut to six minutes. As soon as he finished, his day got even worse.

At the end of the stage, French reporters screaming that he had tested positive for drugs and asking for a comment surrounded Lance. He told the reporters that there must have been some sort of mistake, and that he would get back to them once he found out what had happened. It turned out that Lance was prone to getting sores from riding, and he used a cream to help them heal. The cream had a drug in it, cortisone, which could be confused with steroids in a drug test. Lance had been smart and had made sure to get the race officials' permission to use the cream even before the race started. The race officials were not about to kick Lance out of the race because of the test results. They had recognized the cortisone for what it was, but a reporter had gotten the test results and had printed a story to reflect poorly on Lance.

While Lance should have been resting and preparing for the next day's stage, he was answering these charges. The next stage was one of the toughest in the entire race. It was the Col du Tourmalet, the last big climb of the race. The mountain was so tall that its peak often disappeared into the clouds, as it did on the day of that stage. The cyclists, by the time they reached the summit, were in fog so thick that they couldn't see 10 feet in front of them.

Going up the side of a mountain may be the most difficult part of touring the Pyrenees on a bicycle, but going down the other side is the most dangerous part. Going down the steep inclines, racers can reach speeds up to 70 miles per hour.

Lance did not care about winning the stage. He only worried about protecting his overall lead, by staying close enough to those behind him in the overall race to avoid losing too much time. The key was not to crash, so he was very careful in the fog, and very careful during the downhill, including places in the route where the road appeared to be dropping straight down.

He finished the stage and still had his huge overall lead. There was now only one time trial and one stage left and, if he could continue to avoid disaster, his victory in the Tour de France was all but assured. He had been racing for three weeks, over a course more than 2,000 miles long. He had been on his bike almost 87 hours. His lead was a now huge: six minutes and 15 seconds.

But that did not mean that he was enjoying the experience. The Col du Tourmalet stage had lasted five hours. All Lance wanted to do was rest. Instead, just as had been the case following the previous stage, he had to spend two hours answering questions from the press.

All of the questions were about drugs he had never taken. To help Lance out, the International Cycling Union released the results to each of the drug tests Lance had taken during the Tour. The records showed that he had come up clean for each and every one.

The Final Stretch

Lance wanted his mom to be around in case he won, so he arranged for her to fly to France. On the final time trial of the tour she would get to ride in one of the follow-up cars. When his mother arrived Lance first realized just how famous he had become in the United States. Many Americans were learning about the Tour de France for the first time for one reason: an American, who two years before had almost died from cancer, was in the lead.

During the time trial, Lance could feel his nerves acting up. He could still lose the Tour de France. If he crashed and injured himself, all of his hard work would have been for nothing. But he didn't crash. The time trial went perfectly, just like the two time trials before it. He won the trial by nine seconds, becoming only the fourth cyclist in the history of the race to win all three time trials.

Now he knew he would win the Tour de France. There was no serious racing on the final stage of the Tour. It was a ceremonial parade into Paris. Lance ate ice cream while leading the *peloton*. He even allowed reporters to interview him regarding his victory while on his bike during the final stage.

The cyclists went slowly up Paris's main boulevard, the Champs-Elysées. The streets were jammed with fans. Lance was surprised at all of the support he was receiving. Many fans were waving American flags. He even saw one fellow, probably a tourist, holding up a cardboard sign that read: "TEXAS."

Lance crossed the finish line and got off his bike. The sound of the crowd cheering was deafening in his ears. Kik was there right away to greet him. He gave her a big hug and then asked, "Where's mom?"

His mother pushed her way through the crowd to get to him and hugged her son. A guy Lance had never seen before handed Lance an American flag, which he waved proudly. He had made history as the first American cyclist to win the Tour de France for an American team on an American bike.

He found himself in front of a microphone and realized he was expected to say something to the crowd.

Lance fought back his emotions and said, "I'm in shock. I would just like to say one thing: If you ever get a second chance in life for something, you've got to go all the way."

Then he and his teammates were taken by car to a French museum where a huge celebration was held. Lance raised a glass of champagne and thanked his teammates for all of the hard work they had done. He told them that he could not have won without them.

Kik (left), Lance, and Lance's mother Linda celebrate after Lance's win in the 1999 Tour de France. (Associated Press)

"I wore the yellow jersey," he said, "but I figure the only thing that belongs to me is the zipper."

Lance Armstrong was now a superstar in France, America, and around the world—the most famous cyclist ever. And it was not just because he was an American. It was because he was a survivor.

From Paris, Lance and Kik flew to New York City in a Nike private jet. He rang the bell at the New York Stock Exchange to open the day's stock trading. He met with New York's Mayor Rudy Giuliani and millionaire Donald

Trump. He appeared on the morning network news shows. He made an appearance that night on the CBS TV show, *Late Show with David Letterman.*

Lance had indeed made his comeback.

SUPERSTAR

The Tour de France was over and Lance had won, but the biggest event of Lance's year was still to come. He was going to become a father. The baby was due in the middle of October.

At the start of that month Lance and Bill Stapleton, who was once again his agent, went to Las Vegas where Lance had to attend a series of business meetings and give a speech. When those were finished he flew to Dallas, where he called Kik. She told him that she was having contractions. The baby was on its way. Lance and Bill Stapleton quickly boarded a plane to Austin. Once at the airport Lance got in his car and drove at top speed to meet Kik at St. David's Hospital, the same place where he had had his first cancer surgery.

Difficult Delivery

Lance arrived in time to be in the delivery room, but the birth was not an easy one. The baby came out backward, bottom

Lance, Kik, and Luke.
(www.cycleofhope.org)

rather than headfirst. Doctors had to use a suction device to pull the baby out. In most cases the doctor gives the baby a little whack on the butt to make it cry and clear out its breathing passages. However, once delivered, Lance and Kik's baby did not cry. A tiny oxygen mask was put over the boy's face. After a few moments, which seemed like an eternity to the anxious parents, the mask was removed. The baby let out a long, hard cry and everyone relaxed. Luke David Armstrong, born on October 12, was going to be all right.

Not long after Luke was born, Lance learned that Wheaties, the breakfast cereal, was going to put him on the cover of its boxes. Lance asked if they could hold the press conference announcing the new Wheaties box at the St. David's Hospital children's cancer ward, and the company's representatives agreed.

Doing It Again

With one Tour de France victory under his belt, there was nothing left for Lance to do but to win it again. Lance knew that this time winning would be more difficult. There were a few reasons for this.

For starters, Lance's life had become busier since 1999. He was a new dad. Having a baby in the house has a way of cutting into a parent's sleeping time, and sleep is a critical part of an athlete's training.

Also, Lance had been a well-known cyclist in 1999, and a better-known cancer survivor. But now he was very famous. Whereas he used to be able to walk down the street or work out on his bike without being recognized, now his life was interrupted constantly by a steady stream of autograph-seeking strangers. Although he was thankful for the attention, he hoped it would not get in the way of the single-mindedness needed to train for something as tough as the Tour de France.

Another reason winning this Tour would be difficult was that the other teams would be gunning for him. He was not considered a serious contender to win the 1999 Tour until he was already in the lead. He had, to some extent, caught the other cyclists by surprise. There would be no more of that. The other teams were going to be concentrating on making Lance work as hard as possible from the opening stages of the race right up to the finish.

Crash in the Mountains

There was also an unexpected circumstance that made Lance's chance of winning the 2000 Tour very difficult. During May of 2000, Lance had a serious accident while training in the Pyrenees Mountains. It was a hot day and he had removed his helmet, which is something a cyclist should never do while riding. He hit a stone with his front wheel, got a flat tire and plunged headfirst into a brick wall. An ambulance was called. Lance had a terrible headache and the right side of his face was swelling up badly. In the ambulance, attendants put ice on his face and head, trying to get the swelling to go down. He spent the night in the hospital, one eye swelled shut and he developed a nasty black eye. His skull was not fractured, however, and he was allowed to go home.

They say that when you are bucked off a horse, you have to climb right back on. The fear being that if you don't, you will never get back on the horse at all. Since that mountain climb was going to be a part of the 2000 Tour de France, Lance knew that he was going to have to bike over the route where he had had his accident until he got it right. This time, of course, he would wear his helmet.

Being Lance, he was not content to climb the mountain just once that day. When he was done, having gotten past the location of his accident without a problem, he decided that he had not, as he put it, "understood the mountain."

He went back to the start and rode his bike over the mountain a second time. If anyone thought that a victory in the Tour de France was going to make Lance ease up on his training style, that day would have changed his mind. Lance still punished himself harder than any other racer.

Tour Victory Number Two

The 2000 Tour de France, which went around the outside of France in a counterclockwise direction, was one of the most difficult courses ever designed. It was also one of the rainiest races in history. It rained during nine of the first

Lance rides to his second Tour de France victory, 2000.
(Graham Watson)

10 stages. Lance was in 16th place as the race entered the mountains. But in the 10th stage, the first mountain-climb, Lance made up enough time to take the yellow jersey.

He kept the jersey on the rest of the way, and when the tour was over, he once again stood on top of the podium as the winner. This time Kik had a surprise for him. She had dressed little Luke in a tiny yellow jersey for the celebration. Lance posed for photos with his son sitting on his shoulders.

The Sydney Olympics

With another Tour victory behind him, Lance's mind now shifted to the next big event in his racing career: the Summer Olympics in Sydney, Australia.

Lance had taken some time off after the Tour de France before he began training for the Olympics. When he started training again, another accident slowed down his training schedule. The accident occurred on a sharp turn during a mountain climb not far from Nice, France. He was hit head-on by a car and went flying over its hood.

The driver stopped and asked if Lance was okay. He thought he was at first, although he could tell that his bike was badly broken. The frame had broken into three pieces. It was not until the next morning that he realized how badly he had been hurt. His neck and shoulders were killing him. He went to the doctor where an X ray showed

Lance speeds along in the men's individual time trials at the 2000 Summer Olympic Games in Sydney, Australia. (Duomo/CORBIS)

he had broken his neck. He had to take more time off from training while his neck healed. As soon as he could he got back onto his bike, but the injury had thrown his training schedule out of whack.

Lance enjoyed being part of the U.S. Olympic team in Australia. He raced as hard as he could in both of his races, the road race and the time trial. But his performance in both events was disappointing. He finished 13th in the road race, and although he won a bronze medal in the time trial, which meant that he finished third, he knew that he easily could have won both events if it had not been for his broken neck.

At what was meant to be a victory party after his Olympic race, Lance told a group of friends, "I came here to win, and I didn't. I know you expected better. You went the extra mile for me, to come clear out here, and I lost and I'm sorry about that."

But he could not be too disappointed. It was October 2, 2000, the fourth anniversary of his cancer diagnosis, and it was good to be alive.

In the spring of 2001, Lance and Kik received more good news. Kik was once again pregnant, this time with twins, who were due in December.

The Lance Armstrong Building

In 2001 the Nike World Campus in Beaverton, Oregon, opened a new sports facility for its employees. It was called the Lance Armstrong Building. More than 1,000 people showed up for the dedication ceremony, including Lance, Kristin, Luke, and some of Lance's coaches and doctors.

The dedication ceremony was emceed by Nike boss Phil Knight, who, referring to Lance's miraculous recovery from cancer, said, "Lance brings hope."

The new building had an impressive collection of exercise equipment, an Olympic-size pool, a big rock-climbing wall and, best of all for cycling fans, a bike training system with virtual stages from the Tour de France.

Three Straight

In July 2001, Lance won his third consecutive Tour de France. This tied the record set by Greg LeMond for most Tour de France victories by an American. Lance was, however, the first American to win the Tour three times in a row.

Again, it was in the mountains that Lance excelled. He won one stage in the Alps, one in the Pyrenees, and he won the mountain time trial. In fact, it was just after win-

Until 2001, Greg LeMond (center) held the record for the most consecutive Tour de France victories for an American cyclist. Lance tied this record with his third win in 2001, and he would break it with his fourth win in 2002. (Reuters New Media Inc./CORBIS)

ning the mountain time trial that he learned the twins he and Kik were expecting were going to be girls. Kik had been given an ultrasound procedure to determine the gender of the twins. She carried the envelope with the results to the finish line of the mountain time trial, and after Lance was done racing they opened it together.

He first put on the yellow jersey following the 13th stage. He ended up winning by a seven-minute margin over second-place Jan Ullrich.

If any of Lance's competitors were waiting for him to grow bored with the sport, he let them know that they were in for a long wait.

"I love what I do," he said at his victory press conference. "I love the approach, the preparation; I love the race and as long as that stays the same, I'll be around for years."

Isabelle and Grace

In December of 2001 Kik began to have labor contractions and was ready to go to the hospital. As she and Lance were preparing to leave, there was a knock on the door of their Austin home. It was French racing officials who wanted Lance to take a random drug test.

Lance explained that his wife was about to have twins and this was not the best time for the test. But the officials insisted. If Lance refused to take the test at that moment, he would have been banned from racing for two years. So

Lance presents President George W. Bush with a yellow jersey as Kik and Luke look on. (AFP/CORBIS)

Kristin was forced to wait as Lance provided the officials with a urine sample. Finally the couple was able to leave for the hospital, where Kristin gave birth to their twin girls, Isabelle and Grace.

Number Four

In July 2002, Lance won his fourth consecutive Tour de France. He won four stages during the Tour and, as had become his pattern, he made his big move toward the front of the pack in the mountains. Not everything went smoothly: In the seventh stage Lance came very close to crashing, which could have changed history. But he stayed up.

Lance had now established it as a fact: Nobody went up the side of a mountain on a bicycle like Lance Armstrong. He won by more than seven minutes. His job was made a bit easier by the fact that his rival Jan Ullrich was not in the race. Joseba Beloki, who finished third in the 2000 and 2001 Tours, finished second, with a strong Lithuanian rider named Raimondas Rumsas finishing third.

After the race Beloki said, "I struggled against a rider who is the best in the world. I am happy to be in second place behind Armstrong."

Following the final stage in Paris, Lance received a phone call from President George W. Bush, congratulating him.

At the victory press conference Lance said, "It's an honor and it makes me happy to be able to win again. It was a long three weeks. With so many mountains, it was hard on the head as well as the legs. I'm glad it's over."

As usual, he did not forget his teammates: "It's never easy. In cycling, when you have a consistent and complete team, it makes life easier. Frankly, I think we had the best team in the race. The most motivated, the most experienced, that helps me throughout these three weeks. In fact, their job is a lot harder than my job."

This win made Lance one of only five men in history—and the first American ever—to win four Tours in a row. The world waits to see if he will set even more records.

Fame

With his many victories and triumphs, Lance has become the most famous cyclist, and one of the most famous athletes, in the world. But Lance does not particularly like the fact that he is famous. Although he is very proud of his achievements, fame and celebrity are not his goals. In fact, he has been quoted saying, "Fame and autographs aren't healthy. It's not good for you."

Lance also faces challenges, especially on the Tour, because he is an American cyclist. Many French fans do not like the fact that an American has dominated the Tour de France for several years in a row. But Lance is used to dealing with some negativity from the crowd as he bikes his way across France. Like all winners, Lance knows how to focus on his goals and use all kinds of feedback as extra motivation to finish the race.

Dedication

As Lance's story shows, his fame did not come easily. He is such a successful cyclist because he works harder than almost anyone—all of the time. In the average year he will work long hours on his bike in all but about 10 days. It is

Lance and Luke. (www.cycleofhope.org)

common for cyclists to take time off after the Tour de France. They relax, eat well, and maybe put on a couple of pounds. Then, a couple of months before the racing season begins, they get back on their bike and go back to work.

But not Lance. He rides his bike every day, no matter what. Rain or shine. No matter where in the world he is, or how he is feeling, he rides until it hurts. He is on the bike for five hours most days. On what he called "rest days," he cuts back to two hours on the bike. He explains, "I've got to suffer a little bit every day or I'm not happy."

He rides for 30 hours a week, much of it up steep hills. After all, the Tour goes through the mountains every year, and he has to be ready.

In mid-February of every year, Lance moves to his second home in Spain for the final months of preparation for the Tour de France. According to Lance, this is when he begins his serious training. But according to all the other cyclists in the world, Lance only knows one way to train, and that's very seriously.

Lance trains so hard that no one wants to train with him. A few years ago Johan Bruyneel, the director of the U.S. Postal Service cycling team, thought it would be a good idea for some of the other cyclists on the team to train with Lance for the uphill rides. The idea did not work out. Lance trained so hard that the other cyclists wore down and suffered injuries. The experiment hurt rather than helped their performance at the Tour de France. Later, Bruyeel did not insist that Lance ride alone all the time. He allowed the team to train together two out of three days. On the third day Lance had to train alone while the others were given a chance to rest and recover.

In addition to his physical stamina, Lance's successes are due in large part to his studying the racecourse more than anyone else. For example, in April 2003, Lance was competing for the U.S. Postal team in a four-day race in western France called the Circuit de la Sarthe. It was not an important race, but it was very close to the 30-mile course that would be used for the Tour's time trials. So, while prepping for the Circuit, he rode the time-trial course.

Afterward he said, "It looks straight as an arrow, perfect pavement, absolutely west-east with a few deviations through villages for time checks. They set them up in houses in villages. Today there were headwinds, but it's west-east, the start is right on the beach, so I'd think the winds should be from the back. Could be fast, really fast."

Lance is the only cyclist in history to try to memorize the entire Tour de France course before the race begins. He has said, "If somebody called me and said, 'Hey, it's absolutely flat, good pavement, all on one road,' I'd still come. Even if there wasn't a race like the Circuit de la Sarthe, I'd still fly up here and look it over."

As soon as that year's Tour de France route is announced, Lance will travel to France to train. Many cyclists will struggle up the toughest mountain on the course. Lance, however, will have an easier time of it because he's already ridden up that mountain several times. By June, the month before the Tour starts, he will have ridden along the roads for all the stages.

Five in a Row

On March 24, 2003, Lance told the Spanish newspaper *El Periodico* that he had concerns about being in that year's Tour de France. As the United States was preparing to go to war with Iraq in early 2003, the French government made voiced its objection to the war. Then, when the war began, people around the world protested. Anti-American feelings were very strong in many nations.

Regarding racing in the 2003 Tour, Lance said, "I do have fears because of being an American. I'm not going to deny it. There are certain to be people on the roads. The people will be close to me and they could have contact with me. It's one of the differences between my sport and others like football or Formula One [auto racing]. People are in contact with the cyclists."

Lance pointed out that hundreds of miles of road without barriers, much of which is in the mountains and countryside, could not be kept secure. Two days later, in response to Lance's comments, Tour de France officials said they were thinking about increasing security to keep the cyclists safer.

The 2003 Tour de France was the centennial, or 100th anniversary, of the Tour. "They've tried to make the centennial very significant," said Lance. "But if it was the 99th year or the 101st year, it would still be the most important thing of the year for me. The centennial doesn't change the importance for our team or for me as an athlete."

In the months leading up to the 2003 Tour, Lance had other worries in addition to the race. In February of 2003, Lance and Kristin announced that, after five years of marriage, they were separating. They told the press, "We are working through these sensitive issues in the same way we have met other challenges in our life—together with determination and dedication. We may experience a period of time apart from each other as we reflect on our relationship and work to preserve and protect the interests of our family and children." The separation did not last long, however. Lance went to Europe alone to train for the Tour de France and didn't like it one bit. He called Kik and begged her and the kids to come join him. She said yes, and the family was together again. Events changed course, however, when reports came in fall of 2003 that Lance and Kik had decided to get a divorce.

Despite political and personal problems, Lance won the 2003 Tour de France, and he did so in record-setting fashion. He averaged 25.38 miles per hour over the 23-day, 2,125-mile course—the fastest ever. Despite his speed, his margin of victory was his smallest ever. He finished only 61 seconds ahead of second-place Jan Ullrich of Germany.

Lance's journey was not without incident. In the third stage he was involved in a 35-bicycle pile-up, but he managed to avoid injury. A week later, Joseba Beloki took a hard fall while coming down the side of a mountain, breaking his elbow, leg and wrist. The accident took place right in front of Lance, but he managed to swerve around Beloki in the nick of time. Beloki was only 40 seconds behind Lance for the overall lead at the time. Several times the peloton had to get around groups of protesters demonstrating over issues of local politics. The weather was the hottest for any Tour ever. Temperatures got as high as 103 degrees. Lance fell 93 miles into the 99-mile 15th stage in the Pyrenees mountains. His fall came when a spectator's outstretched bag caught his handlebars. Lance landed on his elbow and shoulder but was unhurt and immediately got back on his bike.

After the stage, Lance said, "After the fall, I had a big rush of adrenaline. I told myself, 'Lance, if you want to win the Tour de France, do it today.'" He went on to win the stage and lengthen his overall lead. The outcome of the race was in doubt until the next-to-final stage when Ullrich fell. He got up immediately and continued on, but his chances of catching Armstrong were gone.

After the race, Ullrich said, "I delivered one of my best races ever. This time I was very close to Armstrong."

Atop the podium, after the "Star-Spangled Banner" was played, Lance exclaimed: "It's a dream, really a dream. I love cycling. I love my job. I will be back for a sixth."

(www.cycleofhope.org)

Looking Forward

Since the Tour began in 1903, only four riders have won it five times, although not in a row. They are: Jacques Anqueil (1957, 1961–1964), Armstrong's buddy Eddy Merckx (1969–1972, 1974), Bernard Hinault (1978, 1979, 1981, 1982, 1985). Lance's five straight victories in the Tour de France tied the record set by Miguel Induráin (1991–1995). Induráin lost trying for his sixth straight win and promptly retired, never to race again. If Lance wins the next Tour, he will set a new world record.

Many wonder if Lance will get off the bike for good if he does not win the 2004 Tour. Although this is a possibility, an end to Lance's cycling career will never end the race of his life. He'll just switch to something else he could do fast. For example, Lance once told a reporter, "I'd love to go into space. I don't know if they'd let me, but that would be a real adventure. The preparation would be cool. There'd be some fun suffering in that, don't you think?"

The Lance Armstrong Foundation has raised more than $23 million to help fight cancer. Thinking back to his illness and the way his experience with cancer changed him forever, Lance says, "It's ironic, I used to ride my bike to make a living. Now I just want to live so that I can ride."

TIME LINE

1971 Lance is born on September 18, near Dallas, Texas, to Linda Mooneyham.

1979 Gets first bicycle, a brown Schwinn Mag Scrambler with yellow wheels

1984 Wins the Iron Kids Triathlon

1988 Earns $20,000 from different types of racing

1989 Trains with the United States Olympic bicycling team in Colorado Springs, Colorado; competes in the Junior World Championships in Moscow

1990 Joins the U.S. national cycling team; wins the Settimana Bergamasca, a 10-day race through the mountains of northern Italy

1991 Becomes U.S. amateur cycling champion

1992   Races in the 1992 Summer Olympics in Barcelona, finishes 14th; afterward turns professional and races for U.S. Team Motorola

1993   Wins the Thrift Drugs "Triple Crown of Racing," and receives $1 million; competes in his first Tour de France, becoming the youngest cyclist ever to win a stage of that race; wins the World Championships in Oslo and, with his mother, gets to meet the king of Norway

1996   Diagnosed with cancer; undergoes two operations and four cycles of chemotherapy

1997   Meets Kristin "Kik" Richard, his future wife; announces comeback to bicycle racing; organizes anti-cancer Ride for the Roses which raises $200,000; joins U.S. Postal Service racing team

1998   Marries Kristin on May 8, in Santa Barbara, California; wins his own race, the Ride for the Roses, in Austin, Texas; returns to Europe and wins the Tour of Luxembourg

1999   In July wins Tour de France for the first time; Kristin gives birth to the couple's first child, Luke David Armstrong, on October 12.

2000   Wins second Tour de France; in October races in Summer Olympics in Sydney, Australia, wins bronze medal

2001   Wins third consecutive Tour de France; in December Kristin gives birth to twins, Isabelle and Grace.

2002   Wins fourth consecutive Tour de France

2003   Wins fifth consecutive Tour de France

HOW TO BECOME A FUND-RAISER

THE JOB

Fund-raisers develop and coordinate the plans by which charity organizations gain financial contributions, generate publicity, and fulfill fiscal objectives. Organized fund-raising, or philanthropy, is a relatively modern refinement of the old notion of charity. It may be surprising to learn that some people make a living by organizing charity appeals and fund drives, but philanthropy ranks among the 10 largest industries in the United States. The most familiar forms of fund-raising are the much publicized and visible types, such as telethons, direct-mail campaigns, and canned food drives. Successful fund-raising does not depend on a high profile; however, it often requires marketing the appeal for funds to the people most likely to donate. Fund-raisers are employed at a variety of nonprofit organizations, including those in the arts, social service, health care, and educational fields, as well as at private consulting firms around the country.

The Lance Armstrong Foundation is a nonprofit organization whose purpose is to enhance the quality of life for people and families living with cancer. The Foundation teaches people how to survive the disease and its effects through individual and community education programs, public advocacy initiatives to improve health care legislation, and grants for cancer research. An important step toward attaining these goals is fund-raising.

Fund-raising careers combine many different skills, such as financial management and accounting, public relations, marketing, human resources, management, and media communications. To be successful, the appeal for funds has to target the people most likely to donate, and donors have to be convinced of the good work being done by the cause they are supporting. To do this, fund-raisers need strong media support and savvy public relations. Fund-raisers also have to bring together people, including volunteers, paid staff, board members, and other community contacts, and direct them toward the common goal of enriching the charity.

To illustrate how a revenue-raising campaign might be conducted, take a look at Branton Academy, a private high school that is trying to raise money to build a new facility. The principal of Branton approaches a fund-raising consulting firm to study the possible approaches to take. Building a new facility and acquiring the land would cost the academy approximately $800,000. The fund-raising firm's first job is to ask difficult questions about the realism of the academy's goal. What were the results of the academy's last fund-raising effort? Do the local alumni tend to respond to solicitations for revenue? Are the alumni active leaders in the community, and can their support be counted on? Are there enough potential givers besides alumni in the area to reach the goal? Are there enough volunteers on hand to launch a revenue campaign? What kind of publicity, good and bad, has the academy recently generated? What other charities, especially private schools, are trying to raise money in the area at that time?

Once the fund-raising consulting firm has a solid understanding of what the academy is trying to accomplish, it conducts a feasibility study to determine whether there is community support for such a project. If community support exists—that is, if it appears that the fund-raising drive could be a success—the consulting firm works with officials at Branton to draft a fund-rais-

106 • *Lance Armstrong: Cyclist*

ing plan. The plan will describe in detail the goals of the fund-raising appeal, the steps to be taken to meet those goals, the responsibilities of the paid staff and volunteers, budget projections for the campaign, and other important policies. For Branton Academy, the fund-raising consultant might suggest a three-tiered strategy for the campaign: a bicycle marathon by the students to generate interest and initiate the publicity campaign, followed by a monthlong phone drive to people in the area, and ending with a formal dinner dance that charges $50 or more per person.

Once the plan is agreed upon, the fund-raising consultants organize training for the volunteers, especially those in phone solicitation, and give them tips on how to present the facts of the campaign to potential contributors and get them to support Branton's efforts. The fund-raisers make arrangements for publicity and press coverage, sometimes employing a professional publicist, so that people will hear about the campaign before they are approached for donations. During the campaign, the consultants and the staff of Branton will research possible large contributors, such as corporations, philanthropic foundations, and wealthy individuals. These potential sources of revenue will receive special attention and personal appeals from fund-raising professionals and Branton's principal and trustees. If the fund-raising effort is a success, Branton Academy will have both the funds it needs to expand and a higher profile in the community.

This example is fairly clear and straightforward, but the financial needs of most charities are so complex that a single, monthlong campaign would be only part of their fund-raising plans. The American Cancer Society, for instance, holds many charity events in an area every year, in addition to occasional phone drives, marathons, year-round magazine and television advertising, and special appeals to large individual donors. The Lance Armstrong Foundation's major fund-raising effort is the Peloton Project, in which cyclists, cancer survivors, and volunteers raise money for the Foundation through bike races (such as the annual Race for the Roses weekend) and community outreach programs.

Fund-raisers who work on the staff of charities and non-profit organizations may need to push several fund drives at the same time, balancing their efforts between long-range endowment funds and special projects. Every nonprofit organization has its own unique goals and financial needs; therefore, fund-raisers have to tailor their efforts to the characteristics of the charity or organization involved. This requires imagination, versatility, and resourcefulness on the fund-raiser's part. The proper allocation of funds is also a weighty responsibility. Fund-raisers also must have strong people skills, especially communications, because their personal contact with volunteers, donors, board members, community groups, local leaders, and members of the press may be an important factor in the success of any revenue appeal.

REQUIREMENTS
High School
To pursue a career in fund-raising, you should follow a college-preparatory curriculum. English, creative writing, speech, mathematics, business, and history classes are recommended, as well as a foreign language, bookkeeping, and computer training. Extracurricular activities such as student council and community outreach programs can help you cultivate important leadership qualities and give you a taste of what fund-raising work requires.

Postsecondary Training
Fund-raising is not a curriculum taught in school, either in high school or at the university level. However, colleges are increasingly offering courses in the broader field of philanthropy. Most fund-raisers have earned a university degree. A broad liberal arts background, with special attention to the social sciences, is a great benefit to fund-raisers because of the nature of most fund-raising

work. Specialized degrees that could benefit fund-raisers include communications, psychology, sociology, public relations, business administration, education, and journalism. This type of education will give fund-raisers insight into the concerns and efforts of most nonprofit organizations and how to bring their worthwhile efforts to the public's attention. Courses in economics, accounting, and mathematics are also very useful.

Certification or Licensing

While not required, CFRE International offers a Certified Fundraising Executive Program. This certification process is endorsed by leading philanthropic associations, including the Association of Fundraising Professionals. Those who hold certification must become recertified every three years.

Other Requirements

Because fund-raisers need to be able to talk and work with all kinds of people, you will need to be outgoing and friendly. Leadership is also an important quality, because you need to gain the respect of volunteers and inspire them to do their best. Their enthusiasm for a campaign can be a major factor in other people's commitment to the cause.

EXPLORING

The best way to gauge your interest in a fund-raising career is to volunteer to help at churches, social agencies, health charities, schools, and other organizations for their revenue drives. All of these groups are looking for volunteers and gladly welcome any help they can get. You will be able to observe the various efforts that go into a successful fund-raising drive and the work and dedication of professional fund-raisers. In this way, you can judge whether you enjoy this type of work. Try to interview the fund-raisers that you meet for their advice in ways to gain more experience and find employment.

EMPLOYERS

Fund-raisers are usually employed in one of three different ways. They may be members of the staff of the organization or charity in question. For example, many colleges and hospitals maintain fund-raisers on staff, sometimes referred to as *solicitors,* who report to the development director or outreach coordinator. They may also be employed by fund-raising consulting firms, which for a fee will help nonprofit organizations manage their campaigns, budget their money and resources, determine the feasibility of different revenue programs, and counsel them in other ways. Many for-profit companies also have fund-raisers on staff to plan and conduct charity social events, such as fund-raising balls, formal dinners, telethons, walk-a-thons, parties, or carnivals. Corporations perform these philanthropic functions both to help the charity and the community and to generate favorable publicity for themselves.

STARTING OUT

The key to a job in fund-raising is experience. Both private consultants and nonprofit staffs prefer to hire fund-raisers who already have worked on other revenue drives. Because their budgets are always tight, nonprofit organizations are especially reluctant to hire people who need to be trained from scratch. Some small organizations that do not have a budget for hiring full-time fund-raisers may use volunteers.

Colleges offer many opportunities for experience, because nearly every college has at least one staff member (more than likely an entire office) in charge of generating donations from alumni and other sources. These staff members will have useful advice to give on their profession, including private consulting firms that hire fund-raisers. A student may have to serve as a volunteer for such a firm first to get to know the people involved and be considered for a permanent position.

ADVANCEMENT

In a private consulting firm, fund-raisers can advance to higher-paying jobs by gaining experience and developing skills. As responsibilities increase, fund-raisers may be put in charge of certain aspects of a campaign, such as the direct mail or corporate appeal, or may even direct an entire campaign. Those who work for a large social service or nonprofit agency will also find that promotions are determined by skill and creativity in handling difficult assignments. After gaining experience with several nonprofit agencies, some fund-raisers move on and start counseling businesses of their own.

EARNINGS

While beginning fund-raisers do not earn much ($20,000 to $25,000), their salaries will increase as they gain experience or lead successful revenue efforts. Fundraisers with 10 to 14 years of experience earned a median annual salary of $54,000 in 2000, according to a membership survey conducted by the Association of Fundraising Professionals. The survey also reports that members who held the Certified Fundraising Executive designation earned median salaries that ranged from $60,000 to $75,000. Experienced fund-raisers can be very highly paid, and some of the best earn more than $200,000 a year. To attract and retain experienced fund-raisers, private agencies and nonprofit organizations will also offer competitive salaries and good benefits. While some nonprofit organizations may offer performance bonuses, they are not usually tied directly to the amounts raised.

Benefits for fund-raisers often are equivalent to other professional business positions, including paid vacation, group insurance plans, and paid sick days.

WORK ENVIRONMENT

The working conditions for professional fund-raisers can sometimes be less than ideal. During revenue campaigns, they may have to work in temporary facilities. Their working hours can be irregular, because they have to meet and work with volunteers, potential donors, and other people whenever those people are available. When campaigns become intense, fund-raisers may have to work long hours, seven days a week. With all the activity that goes on during a campaign, the atmosphere may become stressful, especially as deadlines draw near. So many demands are put on fund-raisers during a campaign—to arrange work schedules, meet with community groups, track finances, and so on—that they must be very organized, flexible, and committed to the overall strategy for the appeal.

OUTLOOK

The job prospects of people who wish to become fund-raisers are good. As federal funding of nonprofit organizations continues to decrease, these groups have to raise operating revenue themselves. They are discovering that hiring full-time fund-raisers is a smart investment. Private fund-raising counseling firms have also reported a need for skilled employees. These firms usually require some experience, but since there are so many fund-raising causes that will eagerly welcome volunteers, interested people should have no problem gaining experience. Both public agencies and private consulting firms keep a full-time staff of fund-raisers, and they may hire part-time workers during special periods and campaigns.

TO LEARN MORE ABOUT FUND-RAISERS

BOOKS

Barksdale, Brent, and Joe Garecht. *25 Fundraising Secrets.* Collierville, Tenn.: Fundcraft Publishing, 2002.

Grimm, Robert T. *Notable American Philanthropists: Biographies of Giving and Volunteering.* Westport, Conn.: Oryx Press, 2002.

Klein, Kim. *Fundraising for Social Change.* San Francisco: Jossey-Bass, 2000.

Lewis, Barbara A., and Pamela Espeland. *The Kid's Guide to Service Projects: Over 500 Service Ideas for Young People Who Want to Make a Difference.* Minneapolis, Minn.: Free Spirit Publishing, 1995.

WEBSITES

American Association of Fundraising Counsel

www.aafrc.org

This organization is a coalition of consulting firms working in the nonprofit sector.

Association of Fundraising Professionals

www.afpnet.org

AFP is a professional association for individuals responsible for generating philanthropic support for nonprofits. It provides educational programs, a resource center, conference, and quarterly journal.

Chronicle of Philanthropy

www.philanthropy.com

A bi-weekly newspaper about fund-raising and philanthropy

CFRE International

www.cfre.org

Offers information on certification as a certified fundraising executive

WHERE TO WRITE

American Association of Fundraising Counsel

10293 North Meridian Street, Suite 175

Indianapolis, IN 46290

Association of Fundraising Professionals

1101 King Street, Suite 700

Alexandria, VA 22314

CFRE International

2815 Duke Street

Alexandria, VA 22314

HOW TO BECOME A PROFESSIONAL ATHLETE

THE JOB

Professional athletes can participate in team sports, such as baseball, basketball, and football, or in individual sports such as cycling, tennis, figure skating, golf, running, or boxing. Professional athletes compete against other athletes or teams to win prizes and money. Here we will focus mainly on becoming a professional athlete in an individual sport.

Depending on the nature of the specific sport, most athletes compete against a field of individuals. The field of competitors can be as small as one (tennis, boxing) or as large as the number of qualified competitors, anywhere from six to 30 (figure skating, golf, cycling). In certain individual events, such as the marathon or triathlon, the field may seem excessively large—often tens of thousands of runners compete in the New York City Marathon—but for the professional runners competing in the race, only a handful of other runners represent real competition.

The athletic performances of those in individual sports are evaluated according to the nature and rules of each specific sport. For example, the winner of a foot race is whoever crosses the finish line first; in tennis the winner is the one who scores the highest in a set number of games; in boxing and figure skating the winners are determined by a panel of judges. Competitions are organized by local, regional, national, and international organizations and associations whose primary functions are to promote the sport and sponsor competitive events. Within a professional sport there are usually different levels of competition based on age, ability, and gender. There are often different designations and events within one sport. Tennis, for example, consists of doubles and singles, while track and field contains many different events, from field events such as the javelin and shot put, to track events such as the 100-meter dash and the two-mile relay race.

Athletes train year-round, on their own or with a coach, friend, parent, or trainer. In addition to stretching and exercising the specific muscles used in any given sport, athletes concentrate on developing excellent eating and sleeping habits that will help them remain in top condition throughout the year. Although certain sports have a particular season, most professional athletes train rigorously all year, varying the type and duration of their workouts to develop strength, cardiovascular ability, flexibility, endurance, speed, and quickness, as well as to focus on technique and control. Often an athlete's training focuses less on the overall game or program that the athlete will execute than on specific areas or details of that game or program. Figure skaters, for example, won't simply keep going through their entire long programs from start to finish but instead will focus on the jumps, turns, and hand movements that refine the program. Similarly, sprinters don't run only the sprint distances they race in during a meet; instead, they vary their workouts to include some distance work, some sprints, a lot of weight training to build strength, and maybe some mental exercises to build control and focus while in the starter's blocks. Tennis players routinely spend hours just practicing their forehand, down-the-line shots.

Athletes often watch videotapes or films of their previous practices or competitions to see where they can improve their performance. They also study what the other competitors are doing in order to prepare strategies for winning.

REQUIREMENTS

High School

A high school diploma will provide you with the basic skills you will need in your long climb to becoming a professional athlete. Business and mathematics classes will teach you how to manage money wisely. Speech classes will help you become a better communicator. Physical education classes will help you build your strength, agility, and competitive spirit. You should, of course, participate in every organized sport that your school offers and that interests you.

Some individual sports such as tennis and gymnastics have professional competitors who are high school students. Teenagers in this situation often have private coaches with whom they practice both before and after going to school, and others are homeschooled as they travel to competitions.

Postsecondary Training

There are no formal education requirements for sports, although certain competitions and training opportunities are only available to those enrolled in four-year colleges and universities. Collegiate-level competitions are where most athletes in this area hone their skills; they may also compete in international or national competitions outside of college, but the chance to train and receive an education isn't one many serious athletes refuse. In fact, outstanding ability in athletics is the way many students pay for their college educations. Given the chances of striking it rich financially, an education (especially a free one) is a wise investment and one fully supported by most professional sports organizations.

Other Requirements

There is so much competition to be among the world's elite athletes in any given sport that talent alone isn't the primary requirement. Diligence, perseverance, hard work, ambition, and courage are all essential qualities to the individual who dreams of making a career as a professional athlete. "If you want to be a pro, there's no halfway. There's no three-quarters way," says Eric Roller, a former professional tennis player who competed primarily on the Florida circuit. Other specific requirements will vary according to the sport. Jockeys, for example, are usually petite men and women.

EXPLORING

If you are interested in pursuing a career in professional sports you should start participating in that sport as much and as early as possible. With some sports, an individual who is 15 may already be too old to realistically begin pursuing a professional career. By playing the sport and by talking to coaches, trainers, and athletes in the field, you can ascertain whether you like the sport enough to make it a career, determine if you have enough talent, and gain new insight into the field. You can also contact professional organizations and associations for information on how to best prepare for a career in their sport. Sometimes there are specialized training programs available, and the best way to find out is to get in contact with the people whose job it is to promote the sport.

EMPLOYERS

Professional athletes who compete in individual sports are not employed in the same manner as most workers. They do not work for employers, but choose the competitions or tournaments they wish to compete in. For example, a professional runner may choose to enter the Boston Marathon and then travel to Atlanta for the Peachtree Road Race.

STARTING OUT

Professional athletes must meet the requirements established by the organizing bodies of their respective sport.

Sometimes this means meeting a physical requirement such as age, height, or weight; sometimes it means fulfilling a number of required stunts, or participating in a certain number of competitions. Professional organizations usually arrange it so that athletes can build up their skills and level of play by participating in lower-level competitions. College sports, as mentioned above, are an excellent way to improve one's skills while pursuing an education.

ADVANCEMENT

Professional athletes advance into the elite numbers of their sport by working and practicing hard, and by winning. Professional athletes usually obtain representation by *sports agents* in the behind-the-scenes deals that determine for which teams they will be playing and what they will be paid. These agents also may be involved with other key decisions involving commercial endorsements, personal income taxes, and financial investments of the athlete's revenues.

A college education can prepare all athletes for the day when their bodies can no longer compete at the top level, whether because of age or an unforeseen injury. Every athlete should be prepared to move into another career, related to the world of sports or not.

EARNINGS

The U.S. Department of Labor reports that athletes had median annual earnings of $43,370 in 2001. Ten percent earned less than $13,610.

Salaries, prize monies, and commercial endorsements will vary from sport to sport; a lot depends on the popularity of the sport and its ability to attract spectators, or on the sport's professional organization and its ability to drum up sponsors for competitions and prize money. Still other sports, like boxing, depend on the skill of the fight's promoters to create interest in the fight. An elite professional tennis player who wins Wimbledon, for example, usually earns over half a million dollars in a matter of several hours. Add to that the incredible sums a Wimbledon champion can make in endorsements and the tennis star can earn over $1 million a year. This scenario is misleading, however; to begin with, top athletes usually cannot perform at such a level for very long, which is why a good accountant and investment counselor comes in handy. Secondly, for every top athlete who earns millions of dollars in a year, there are hundreds of professional athletes who earn less than $40,000. The stakes are incredibly high, the competition fierce.

Perhaps the only caveat to the financial success of an elite athlete is the individual's character or personality. An athlete with a bad temper or prone to unsportsmanlike behavior may still be able to set records or win games, but he or she won't necessarily be able to cash in on commercial endorsements. Advertisers are notoriously fickle about the spokespeople they choose to endorse products; some athletes have lost million-dollar accounts because of their bad behavior on and off the field of play.

Other options exist for the professional athlete who has reached the end of his or her career. Many go into some area of coaching, sports administration, management, or broadcasting. The professional athlete's unique insight and perspective can be a real asset in careers in these areas. Other athletes have been simultaneously pursuing other interests, some completely unrelated to their sport, such as education, business, social welfare, or the arts. Many continue to stay involved with the sport they have loved since childhood, coaching young children or volunteering with local school teams.

WORK ENVIRONMENT

Athletes compete in many different conditions, according to the setting of the sport (indoors or outdoors) and the rules of the organizing or governing bodies. Track-and-field athletes often compete in hot or rainy conditions, but at any point organizing officials can call off the meet or postpone competition until better weather. Indoor events are less subject to cancellation. However, since it is in the best interests of an organization not to risk the athletes' health, any condition that might adversely affect the outcome of a competition is usually reason enough to cancel or postpone it. An athlete, on the other hand, may withdraw from competition if he or she is injured or ill. Nerves and fear are not good reasons to default on a competition, and part of ascending into the ranks of professional athletes means learning to cope with the anxiety that competition brings. Some athletes actually thrive on the nervous tension.

In order to reach the elite level of any sport, athletes must begin their careers early. Most professional athletes have been working at their sports since they were small children; skiers, figure skaters, and gymnasts, for example, begin skiing, skating, and tumbling as young as age two or three. Athletes have to fit hours of practice time into an already full day, usually several hours before school, and several hours after school. To make the situation more difficult, competitions and facilities for practice are often far from the young athlete's home, which means they either commute to and from practice and competitions with a parent, or they live with a coach or trainer for most of the year. Separation from a child's parents and family is an especially hard and frustrating element of the training program. When a child has demonstrated uncommon excellence in a sport, the family often decides to move to the city in which the sports facility is located, so that the child doesn't have to travel or be separated from a normal family environment.

The expenses of a sport can be overwhelming, as can the time an athlete must devote to practice and travel to and from competitions. In addition to specialized equipment and clothing, the athlete must pay for a coach, travel expenses, competition fees, and, depending on the sport, time at the facility or gym where he or she practices. Tennis, golf, figure skating, and skiing are among the most expensive sports to enter.

Even with the years of hard work, practice, and financial sacrifice that most athletes and their families must endure, there is no guarantee that an athlete will achieve the rarest of the rare in the sports world—financial reward. An athlete needs to truly love the sport at which he or she excels, and also have a nearly insatiable ambition and work ethic.

OUTLOOK

Again, the outlook will vary depending on the sport, its popularity, and the number of professional athletes currently competing. On the whole, the outlook for the field of professional sports is healthy, but the number of jobs will not increase dramatically. Some sports, however, may experience a rise in popularity, which will translate into greater opportunities for higher salaries, prize monies, and commercial endorsements.

TO LEARN MORE ABOUT PROFESSIONAL CYCLISTS AND OTHER ATHLETES

BOOKS

Armstrong, Lance, Chris Carmichael, and Peter Joffre Nye. *The Lance Armstrong Performance Program: Seven Weeks to the Perfect Ride.* Emmaus, Pa.: Rodale Press, 2000.

Burke, Ed R. *The Complete Book of Long-Distance Cycling.* Emmaus, Pa.: Rodale Press, 2000.

Carmichael, Chris, and Jim Rutberg. *The Ultimate Ride: Get Fit, Get Fast, and Start Winning with the World's Top Cycling Coach.* New York: Putnam, 2003.

Jeukendrup, Asker E. *High-Performance Cycling.* Champaign, Ill.: Human Kinetics Publishers, 2002.

CYCLING WEBSITES

Cycling Hall of Fame

www.cyclinghalloffame.com

Tributes to the all-time greatest cyclists

International Cycling Union

www.uci.ch

A good general information site about the world of cycling

USA Cycling Online

www.usacycling.org

News about cycling events, equipment, and clubs

The World Center of Cycling

www.cyclingnews.com

Schedules and results of major races around the world

GENERAL ATHLETIC WEBSITES

The best way to learn about becoming a professional athlete is to contact the professional organizations for the sport in which you would like to compete, such as the National Tennis Association, the Professional Golf Association, or the National Bowling Association. The following organizations provide helpful information on a variety of sports topics.

American Alliance for Health, Physical Education, Recreation, and Dance

www.aahperd.org

This site is a good source of information on requirements, training centers, and coaches for various sports.

Amateur Athletic Union

www.aausports.org

The AAU can provide you with a free brochure and information on the Junior Olympics and more.

WHERE TO WRITE

American Alliance for Health, Physical Education, Recreation, and Dance

1900 Association Drive
Reston, VA 20191-1598

Amateur Athletic Union

PO Box 22409
Lake Buena Vista, FL 32830

TO LEARN MORE ABOUT LANCE ARMSTRONG

BOOKS

Abt, Samuel and James Startt. *Lance Armstrong's Comeback from Cancer: A Scrapbook of the Tour de France Winner's Dramatic Career.* San Francisco: Van der Plas Publications, 1999.

Armstrong, Lance, and Sally Jenkins. *It's Not About the Bike: My Journey Back to Life.* New York: Berkley Books, 2001.

Armstrong, Kristin. *Lance Armstrong: The Race of His Life.* New York: Grosset & Dunlap, 2000.

Christopher, Matt. *On the Bike With...Lance Armstrong.* New York: Little, Brown, 2003.

Garcia, Kimberly. *Lance Armstrong.* Bear, Del.: Mitchell Lane Publishers, 2003.

Gutman, Bill. *Lance Armstrong: A Biography.* New York: Pocket Books, 2003.

Pavelka, Ed (ed.). *Bicycling Magazine's Complete Book of Road Cycling Skills.* Emmaus, Pa.: Rodale Press, 1998.

Stewart, Mark. *Sweet Victory: Lance Armstrong's Incredible Journey.* Madison, Wis.: Turtleback Books, 2000.

Thompson, John. *Lance Armstrong.* Broomall, Pa.: Chelsea House, 2001.

Watson, Graham. *Lance Armstrong and the 1999 Tour de France.* Boulder, Colo.: Velo Press, 1999.

NEWSPAPERS AND MAGAZINES

Reilly, Rick, "Sportsman of the Year: Lance Armstrong," *Sports Illustrated*, December 16, 2002, pp. 52-71.

Abt, Samuel. "Tour Is Not Until July, but Don't Tell Armstrong." *New York Times*, April 13, 2003, Section 8, p. 12.

WEBSITES

Lance Armstrong's Official Website

www.lancearmstrong.com

All the latest for Lance fans

Louisiana-Mississippi Bicycle Racing Association Website

www.bicycleracing.com

Links to information about bike manufacturers, events, clubs, and coaches

Pro Cycling's Internet Hall of Fame

http://townsleyb.members.beeb.net/procycle/
  Indexfrm.htm

A collection of information about the greatest pro cyclists from 1950 to the present

INTERESTING PLACES TO VISIT

Bicycle Museum of America

7 West Monroe Street (State Route 274)

New Bremen, OH 45869

(419) 629-9249

www.bicyclemuseum.com

Dedicated to the history of cycling in America

United States Bicycling Hall of Fame

145 West Main Street

P.O. Box 853

Somerville, NJ 08876

(908) 722-3620

www.usbhof.com

Call first as the organization is planning to move.

INDEX

Page numbers in *italics* indicate illustrations.

A

accidents
  Nice, France 84–85
  1999 racing season 64–65
  playing "chicken" 14
  Pyrenees mountains, training 82
  Tour de France, 1995 35–38
Amstel Gold Race 66–67
Anqueil, Jacques 98
Armstrong, Grace 88–89
Armstrong, Isabelle 88–89
Armstrong, Kristin (Richard) *80*
  childbirth 79–80, 88–89
  engagement 58
  France, move to 59–60, 63–64
  meeting 54
  pregnancy 64
  separation 96
  Spain vacation 56
  Tour de France, 1999 76, *77*
  Tour de France, 2000 83
  wedding 62–63
Armstrong, Lance *61, 80, 87. See also
  specific topic*
  books on and by 133–134
  "Bull of Texas" 18
  cancer, bout with 39–53
  comeback after cancer 54–78
  dedication 91–94

early life 3–16
Europe, unpopularity 22–23
fame 91
France, move to 59–60, 63–64
learning more about 133–135
learning to race 17–27
with Luke *92*
marriage to Kristin (Kik) (*See*
  Armstrong, Kristin (Richard))
newspaper and magazine articles 134
professional, turning 20–22
retirement 60–62
Russia, trip to 15–16
separation 96
superstar status 79–99
swimming 6
timeline 100–102
triathlon 7–10
Triple Crown 23–24
websites 134
Armstrong, Luke *80*
  birth of 79–80
  with Bush, George *89*
  with Lance *92*
  Tour de France, 2000 83
Armstrong, Terry 4–5, 7, 9
Austin, Texas 18, *19*

B

Barcelona, Spain
  1992 Olympics 21
Beloki, Joseba 90, 97

ABOUT THE AUTHOR

Michael Benson has written young-adult biographies of Ronald Reagan, Bill Clinton, William Howard Taft, Malcolm X, Muhammad Ali, Dale Earnhardt, and Gloria Estefan. He is the former editor of *All-Time Baseball Greats*, *Fight Game*, and *Stock Car Spectacular* magazines. He is the author of 30 books, including *The Encyclopedia of the JFK Assassination* and *Complete Idiot's Guides to NASA, The CIA, National Security, Aircraft Carriers, Submarines*, and *Modern China*. Originally from Rochester, N.Y., he is a graduate of Hofstra University. He enjoys his life with his wife and two children in Brooklyn, N.Y., and his goal is to one day write the Great American Novel.